LAUNCH
YOURSELF

A PROVEN METHOD TO DEFINE, DESIGN, AND DELIVER A POWERFUL PERSONAL BRAND **THAT GETS YOU RESULTS.**

KRISTA NEHER

For general information on our other products and for services or technical support please see www.bootcampdigital.com or Contact Customer Care at 513-223-3878.

ISBN-13: 978-0-9830286-6-6

Printed in the United States of America

First Edition

This book is dedicated to you. Build your brand and achieve your dreams.
I can't wait to see what you do with what you learn.

"The most effective way to do it is to do it."

#LaunchYourself

BEFORE YOU START

Get the Action Planner to make the most out of this book.

DOWNLOAD THE PLANNER

Get a *FREE* download of the 55-page Define, Design, and Deliver a Powerful Personal Brand ACTION PLANNER.

+ Free downloads of all resources inside this book!

Go to **www.LaunchYourself.com/Book** to download your *FREE* Action Planner and resources.

PRINT PLANNER + IMPLEMENTATION GUIDES

Get the print version of the planner and the complete Tools and Resources Kit, including:

- LinkedIn Profile Best Practices
- Social Media Quick-Start guides to get you started on LinkedIn, Facebook, Instagram, Twitter, blogging and *more!*
- Checklists to creating great content

Go to **www.LaunchYourself.com/Planner** or Amazon: **Launch Yourself Personal Branding Action Planner**.

GET THE WORKSHOP

Guided step-by-step video training for better results faster. Guaranteed.

The online Launch Yourself! Training gives you everything you need to define, design and deliver a personal brand that attracts the opportunities you want. Krista Neher shows you exactly how to implement everything you learned including:

- Step-by-step tutorials
- Examples
- Personal stories and examples
- How-to implementation advice
- Downloads, tips and tricks
- Motivation and inspiration to get the results you deserve

LaunchYourself! Online Program Includes:

- 8+ Hours of Video Training
- Step-by-step instruction and examples
- Action Planner & Implementation Guide
- 1:1 Coaching with Office Hours
- LinkedIn Masterclass
- *Bonus*: High-Impact Digital Marketing Webinars
- *Bonus*: Digital Marketing Tools Video Tutorials

Go to **www.LaunchYourself.com** to enroll today!

Contact us for custom corporate workshops, keynote presentations and more at **info@bootcampdigital.com** or call us at 513-223-3878.

How to Use This Book

This book is designed to give you an overview of digital marketing strategies, tools, and tactics but also empower you with a solid understanding for implementation. Whether you are a digital marketer, a brand manager, an agency pro, an entrepreneur, a business leader, or a professional wanting to grow your knowledge, this book will put you on the path to success.

To maximize your value from the book, you'll see icons and specific call-outs to draw your attention to elements that are important to your success. You'll see these throughout the book.

Tools
You'll get recommendations on specific tools or resources that you can use to implement.

Power Tip
This is a high-impact tip that can really impact your success and results. These are easy to implement.

Remember
This is an important point that you will want to keep in mind going forward.

Big Idea
This is an idea that is central to the topic and should get you thinking about how to drive your results.

Action Item
We'll draw your attention to things that you should do immediately. (You can also save these to do later!)

Example
Examples that bring the concept to life are highlighted. This helps in implementation.

TABLE OF CONTENTS

INTRODUCTION

I started thinking about my personal brand about 12 years ago. When I got started, I was working for a big Fortune 500 company and I was in the process of a career change. After working in finance for six years, I knew I wanted to switch gears and work in marketing – specifically social media marketing.

There were two big moments that caused me to start thinking about my personal brand. The first was when a coworker googled me (I still have no idea why) and found a photo of me in a bathrobe at a party. In context, the photo was appropriate. I was at an industry pajama party. Out of context, it was questionable.

The second moment was when I received a MySpace friend request from a business contact. Yes, this was pre-Facebook. My MySpace page consisted mostly of inside jokes. Vanilla Ice was in my Top 5 and there were pics of me out with my friends drinking. It wasn't a good professional look. I had started a side-gig of running marketing for an internet startup, and business contacts from events were finding about me on MySpace and attempting to connect.

Between these two moments I had a wake-up call. I needed to think deliberately about the personal brand that I was creating – both in real life and online.

Big Idea
You already have a personal brand. The question is whether or not you decide to control it.

I was in my late 20s and while I wasn't about to remove my entire personal and social life from the internet, I felt that I needed to be more proactive and deliberate about my personal brand. I wanted to have more control over the perceptions that I was creating. I wanted my online brand to work for me.

I started focusing on my online brand – I made a LinkedIn profile, became active on Twitter, and started a blog. I didn't spend too much time or do anything too dramatic. What blew my mind was the immediate results I saw.

After doing marketing for only a year, I had a director-level job offer, that I thought I was TOTALLY not qualified for, from a leading ad agency. I would never have even applied for the job thinking it was out of reach. Instead, they came knocking down my door offering it to me. It amazed me that in only a year I had been able to credibly position myself in an industry and generate job offers beyond what I would have ever applied for.

Big Idea
When you take control of your personal brand you can influence how people perceive you. This positions you to **attract the opportunities you want**.

Fast-forward 5- 10 years and I had created a strong and credible brand for myself. The journey wasn't without hiccups and learnings along the way – my first blog url was thisiswhyimhot.wordpress.com – and that was my attempt to create a credible marketing blog <cringe>.

Remember
You might not get it right the first time. That's ok. Your brand will evolve and you can improve it over time.

2

As I sorted it out and improved little by little each year, my online brand led to some of my biggest professional accomplishments:

- Two book deals
- International speaking
- Impressive client roster
- Job offers
- Media appearances

I remember specifically doing an interview on NPR seven or eight years ago, and afterwards I received a phone call from someone who had heard the interview. She wanted to hire my company for a project. She said she heard me on NPR, googled me, and "couldn't believe that someone like me was based in Cincinnati." She felt "lucky" that she could meet and work with me.

I almost spit out my coffee.

She thought I was a big deal.

Was I a big deal?

The interesting thing about it, was that her **perception** of my qualifications and "big dealness" came from her visiting my website – where *I created the content, the story, and the perception.* I was struck by my ability to design something that left such a strong impression with someone.

I was blown away by the power that I had to craft a perception of myself. Afterwards I started to take inventory of some of my major professional accomplishments, and I realized that most of them were a direct result of my personal brand.

Big Idea
You have the power to craft a personal brand that drives impact. You just have to do it.

Around the same time, I created the first *Launch Yourself* workshop for business professionals. I had been training businesses in social media marketing since 2006, and I realized that many of the people who came to workshops wanted to build **their personal brand,** not just the brand of their business.

When I ran my first personal branding workshops, one of the attendees had just launched his own business after changing careers. Upon googling himself he found that there was very little information that would build confidence that he was an expert in his new field. He updated his profiles and started posting thought leadership content and within six months he was turning away business. His brand was attracting the opportunities he wanted.

My mission is simple. I want to help others to have the same professional success I had with their personal brand. The reality is that there are many very qualified people who don't invest in their personal brands and it limits their success or prevents opportunities from finding them.

A friend of mine actually LOST A JOB opportunity after they googled her online. It wasn't even because of anything that seemed obviously inappropriate. They said that upon further reviewing her online they felt that she lacked the communication skills needed for the role. As a side note, poor communication is one of the top reasons that qualified people lose job opportunities.

But I don't want to just help you to avoid a bad situation.

In this book I will show you exactly how to Define, Design, and Deliver a personal brand that attracts the opportunities you want. This isn't about not posting inappropriate content – this is about crafting a personal brand for yourself where people are excited to work with you. A brand that attracts the opportunities that you want.

 I got a sales call from a financial advisor, and upon googling him I found that we had a lot of mutual connections on LinkedIn and Facebook. He also shared results that his clients were getting and financial articles, that showed his expertise. My mindset changed from "get this guy to leave me alone" to "please come over and help me." He has been my financial advisor for 10 years.

This book will show you how to use the proven strategies that big brands use, as well as online marketing principles to create a powerful personal brand that positions you as a credible expert and attracts the opportunities that you want.

This book has three main sections covering the three stages of executing a stand-out personal brand.

Define: What you are about
Design: Make it compelling and desirable
Deliver: Make it visible

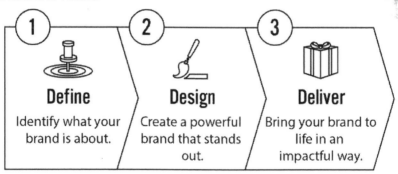

We strongly recommend you download the action planner to accompany this book and make the most out of it at **www.launchyourself.com/book**

PART 1: GETTING STARTED WITH YOUR PERSONAL BRAND

You may already be inspired and excited to get started with your personal brand. This section will help you understand the importance of your personal brand and the impact that in can have on you professionally. Whether you are a public figure, a coach, a consultant, or a business professional you have a personal brand and now is the time to take charge of it.

In the age of the internet your personal brand is more important than ever. There is less separation between personal and professional, public, and private. Your brand is created by everything you do and everything you post, regardless of where you post it. This means that, especially online, it is important to be deliberate.

This section will also explore some "pre-work" to get you thinking about yourself and your personal brand. The idea is to start examining yourself so that you can build on this as you define, design, and deliver your personal brand.

The self-discovery in this section will help you to evaluate yourself, how people perceive you, and your strengths to bring to life as you Launch Yourself. You'll also be inspired to look at others in your industry, field, or who you admire so that you can see how smart, successful professionals are crafting personal brands that get results.

CHAPTER 1: WHAT IS A PERSONAL BRAND?

Your personal brand is the perception that people have about you. You already have a personal brand, whether you like it or not, as everyone you come in to contact with has a perception about you.

The idea of personal branding is to be deliberate about the brand that you create for yourself. It is about building a powerful, positive reputation that attracts opportunities to you.

According to Wikipedia:

> **Personal branding** is the practice of people marketing themselves and their careers as brands. ... **Personal branding** is essentially the ongoing process of establishing a prescribed image or impression in the mind of others about an individual, group, or organization.
>
> Personal branding - Wikipedia
> https://en.wikipedia.org/wiki/Personal_branding

We often think of branding as something that applies to consumer products like Coca-Cola or Starbucks, but people have brands to. A brand is really just the perception that you have of a product or person – and it may be both logical (Apple makes great computers) and emotional (Apple products are cool).

According to Jeff Bezos, Founder of Amazon "Personal brand is what people say about you when you leave the room."

Big Idea
A personal brand is the perceptions that people have about you. These already exist, but the question to ask yourself is if you know what they are?

Consider the differences between the personal brands of Steve Jobs vs. Bill Gates. When people think of Jobs, they think edgy, innovative, design, hip. When they think Gates, they think conservative, dorky, philanthropy, serious. Both Jobs and Gates are selling computers, but they do it with very different personal brands.

The same example could be used to look at Rachael Ray and Martha Stewart. Both are positioning themselves as culinary experts and building strong, powerful brands, yet they each use very different positioning.

Rachael Ray comes across as casual, friendly, funny and is almost like the fun girlfriend or next-door neighbor that you are catching up with.

Martha Stewart, on the other hand, has a more serious and refined brand that feels elevated and superior. It isn't relatable – it is more aspirational. If you look at the tone Ray uses in her posts it is fun and casual – "We've got Rachael's hubby John's fav dish... and made it extra delicious." Stewart takes a more serious and affluent tone. "This classic chicken fricassee turns humble ingredients into a heartiest dinner."

While both are trying to achieve the same thing – a strong personal brand in the culinary space – they each do it in very different ways, and they are both successful.

Different tones, styles, and personalities can be effective at personal branding – but all personal brands harness the same principles of branding to be memorable, authentic, different, and educated.

The idea of online personal branding is to extend your personal brand online in a smart way so you can reach more people more effectively as a business professional.

Big Idea
There are many different personal brand styles that are effective. The key is to determine the brand style that is right for you and your personal brand objectives.

Some people think that a personal brand is about creating a logo, a good profile photo, LinkedIn profile, or website. These are elements of how you bring your brand to life, but a strong personal brand starts before you create any content online.

The best and strong brands (both personal brands and consumer brands) are built based on proven principles that make them memorable, authentic, distinctive, and credible.

If you want to execute a strong strategic personal brand you'll need to do some planning and prioritizing first to discover why you want to create one, what you do and how you position it, the elements to highlight as you bring your brand to life, and then choose the strategic tools to deliver your brand in a consistent and compelling way.

Remember
Taking the time to think through what you want your brand to represent and how you will bring it to life will make for a stronger and more deliberate execution and, ultimately, better results.

This book will take you through all the steps to defining, designing, and delivering a powerful personal brand.

CHAPTER 2: WHY YOUR PERSONAL BRAND MATTERS

People do business with people and brands that they know, like, and trust. This simple age-old sales principle still drives decisions from the laundry detergent we use, car we drive, insurance agent we sign up with, products we buy online, and business coach we hire.

Building know, like, and trust is both a big risk and opportunity in the digital age. The risk happens when people search for you online, assess your credibility, and come up empty, or with less than favorable results. The opportunity is that your digital footprint can be a powerful tool to grow your professional network and your position as an expert, which can ultimately impact your bottom line. And you can control it.

The reality is that people are googling you before, during, and after they meet you. They want to check you out, assess your credibility, see your credentials, consider if you are trustworthy, recommend you to a friend or are maybe just curious.

Your online brand is like the suit you wear to look professional. It is the waiting room of your office. It is your business card. It is your first impression.

When someone searches for you, what will they find?

Of the 75% of US adults who google themselves, nearly half say that the results are not positive (according to Google). Smart business professionals aren't just focusing on building a personal brand that isn't a liability – they are using it as a strategic tool to grow their reputation and business success.

Why YOU Need a
Personal Brand

1 👍 **Establish your reputation**
- 75% of people google other people
- Over half of people aren't happy with their results
- This is your first impression

2 ✍ **Increase your credibility**
- People judge you based on what they find
- Put your best foot forward
- Create WOW!

3 ⭐ **Attract opportunities**
- Grow professional success
- New opportunities come to you
- Take charge of your future

WHAT CAN YOUR BRAND DO FOR YOU?

If you want professional career success – whether it is upward mobility, new job opportunities, increased sales, a stronger network – or if you are the product you are marketing – speakers, authors, coaches, consultants, entrepreneurs – your personal brand is the key to your success.

I've worked with tens of thousands of business professionals on their personal brands, and some of the results they've seen include:

- Job offers
- Promotions
- Sales
- New clients
- Board seats
- Speaking engagements
- Media appearances
- Book deals
- First jobs
- Career changes
- Business leads
- Investment opportunities
- Investors for their startup

Regardless of whether you are a student looking for your first job or a seasoned professional looking to accelerate your success, your personal brand can be the key to unlocking opportunities.

REINVENTING YOURSELF OR CHANGING CAREERS

Business professionals today change employers and even careers more than ever before. One of the most common questions I get about personal branding is how to position yourself or build a brand if you want to change careers or reposition your skills.

First the good news - you can change careers at any point, and a strong personal brand is your key to doing this effectively.

When changing careers your personal brand is even more important, as you need to start to build a perception of yourself in an area that you may not have a lot of skills or experience in.

I successfully changed careers because of my personal brand. I actually started my career in finance and spent six years in that industry prior to switching to marketing. When I decided to make that switch, I didn't have much marketing experience – I had worked in marketing for a startup for a few months, but that was it.

I started a social media presence where I shared what I was doing in social media marketing. I updated my LinkedIn profile and optimized it towards marketing including associations I had joined, my marketing blog, etc. What was amazing to me was that because I talked about social media and **showed my knowledge and results** it didn't seem to matter that I wasn't experienced.

When I look at hiring people today, enthusiasm, demonstrated passion and an online presence showing thought leadership and ideas goes a longer way than experience on a résumé. Smart career-changers embed themselves in an industry and connect with leaders and influencers to build their knowledge and reputation.

If you are changing careers, a personal brand can be your best friend. By *showing* that you have the passion, knowledge, and some experience, you can set yourself apart.

YOUR GOAL ISN'T TO NOT SUCK

When it comes to personal branding, especially online branding many people think that if they don't have anything terrible pop up, they're doing an okay job.

YOUR GOAL ISN'T TO NOT SUCK!

Your goal is to craft an amazing personal brand and online presence that attracts opportunities and makes you desirable.

When someone meets you, they can be **very interested** in you and **excited to work with you.** You can be **mediocre or average** and make a small impression, or you can create a **bad impression.**

Your goal is to create a strong **positive impression** that makes people say "WOW! I would love to work with you!" It may take time to fully get there, but remember, the goal isn't to avoid mistakes and not have anything terrible – the goal is to be amazing – **and you can be!**

krista neher

Web   Images   Maps   Shopping   More ▼   Search tools

About 77,500 results (0.31 seconds)

Krista Neher - Social Media Keynote Speaker - Leading Authority ...
kristaneher.com/ ▼
Krista Neher is an author, professor, keynote speaker and expert on social media.
Krista is an ideal speaker for corporate events, colleges, workshop.
Google+ page · Write a review

 1600 Main St Cincinnati, OH 45202
(646) 450-2267

Contact - Speaking Topics - Krista's Story

Krista Neher (**KristaNeher**) on Twitter
https://twitter.com/KristaNeher ▼
The latest from **Krista Neher** (@**KristaNeher**). CEO Boot Camp Digital marketing
consulting and training. Marketing pro. Entrepreneur. Geek. Connector. Speaker ...

Krista Neher | LinkedIn
www.linkedin.com/in/kristaneher ▼
Cincinnati Area - Marketing strategist, bestselling author, international speaker &
professor on social media, mobile & internet marketing
View **Krista Neher**'s professional profile on LinkedIn. LinkedIn is the world's largest
business network, helping professionals like **Krista Neher** discover inside ...

Krista Neher | ClickZ
www.clickz.com/author/profile/2269/krista-neher ▼
by Krista Neher - in 811 Google+ circles
Krista Neher is the author of the bestselling Social Media Field Guide, an
international speaker, and currently CEO of Boot Camp Digital, which is a
leading ...

Krista Neher LLC

Directions   Write a review

Address: 1600 Main St, Cincinnati, OH 45202
Phone: (646) 450-2267
Transit: Main St & Orchard St

Feedback

Benefits of a Strong
Personal Brand

Regardless of the size of your ambition – whether it is landing the next sale, growing in your current position or becoming an industry thought-leader – your personal brand can launch your professional success.

A strong personal brand...

1 👍 Establishes your reputation

2 🖊 Increases your credibility

3 ☆ Attracts opportunities

What can your brand bring you?

- Book deals
- Speaking
- Clients
- Sale
- Job offers
- Board positions

- Expert opportunities
- Press opportunities
- Become an influencer

- Promotion
- Career change
- Start a business
- Become an industry leader
- Sell a product

CHAPTER 3: THE BEST WAY TO DO IT IS TO DO IT

One of the biggest challenges when it comes to establishing and growing your personal brand is just doing it.

After working with thousands of people on their personal brand the #1 thing that prevents them from being successful is just not executing. Not doing it.

Why don't they do it?

Usually it's fear, uncertainty, and mindset that hold them back.

REASON #1 - FEAR.

Let's face it, putting yourself out there always comes with some fear. What if I sound stupid? What if people don't like what I have to say? What if I come across as too egotistical? Will I seem full of myself? Will people make fun of me?

These are all fears that hold us back from acting. Let go of these.

I remember writing my first blog post and worrying that I didn't sound smart enough. Or that people who knew more than me would think I was wrong.

The reality is that when you speak from experience and knowledge you should have every confidence in what you are doing.

Power Tip
For every person who knows more than you, there are millions of people who know less and can really benefit from what you have to share.

If you let fear hold you back, you are only harming yourself. The reality is that you have a unique perspective and personality and can build an authentic and meaningful brand for yourself. *Don't worry about other people.*

Some people are just negative. Haters gonna hate, am I right? And some people struggle with the success of others. Focus on the positive and remember that most people will cheer and applaud and find value in what you are sharing.

Do it.

REASON #2 - UNCERTAINTY.

The second big reason for not taking action is uncertainty. Personal branding (heck, any kind of branding) is difficult, and you will NEVER have all the answers.

Many people feel paralyzed because they don't have a great, specific definition of what their brand is, or they don't have that perfect headshot.

In a workshop, I had a woman tell me she didn't update her LinkedIn profile because she didn't have a great headshot and she wanted to get professional hair and makeup. Sure, your profile picture is the most important thing, but don't let that hold you back. If you wait for perfect, you will never do it. Get the best picture you can now and get started!

I worked with another friend who waited two years to establish his personal brand because he couldn't decide on his positioning. Think of all the opportunities he lost during that time. He could have just started posting, establishing his presence, and getting some experience around what worked for him and generated a positive response from his audience. Instead he did nothing.

My personal brand is still under construction and always will be. There are some parts that are strong – my credibility and consistency – and others that I still want to improve – my personality and a clearer tone of voice or position.

Don't worry if you don't have all of the answers or if they aren't perfect.

Don't let a lack of perfection or uncertainty hold you back. Spoiler alert, perfection will NEVER come. Get as close as you can and get started. You'll refine and improve your personal brand over time – but only if you START.

Do it.

REASON #3 – MINDSET.

The third reason that people fail to get started a mindset issue – they put more effort into the excuses of why they can't start instead of just starting. Just do it. Just do it. Just do it.

Begin with the things that seem reasonable.

A very good friend of mine is a world-known expert in his field, and he is working to build up his speaking business. He is a GREAT speaker and he even has an agent. But he has a terrible, 10-year-old, amateur website. He knows this. He isn't blind. It is seriously the #1 thing that would get him more opportunities overnight.

Yet he hasn't fixed it? Why not? Mindset.

There is always some "reason" to not do something or to wait. The longer you wait, the longer you miss out.

Generate a bias towards action with your personal brand. Stop waiting and delaying for any reason.

Big Idea
Your brand will continue to evolve over time. As you learn, get feedback, and grow you will refine and improve your brand. Don't hesitate – develop a bias for action.

Just do it.

Your personal brand is an investment that you make in yourself that will pay you dividends throughout your career. Start focusing on it now with the mindset that you'll always be refining.

Action Item
Set yourself a timeline and stick to it as best as you so that you continue to make progress. It's easy to get hung up on some big questions or wanting to make things perfect. Allow yourself some time to get the best answers possible and then move on.

CHAPTER 4: EXPLORE, EXAMINE, AND GET INSPIRED

One of the things that can be most challenging about personal branding is that it is so, well, personal. This means that you need to dig deep inside yourself and hold up a mirror to understand who you are and your strengths.

Often, we don't see ourselves clearly, yet others – coworkers, partners, friends, family, and acquaintances – see things in us that we don't see in ourselves.

Power Tip

Most of the best insights I've gained into my personal brand (positive ideas and opportunities) came from other people. **Ask** for opinions and **be open** to think about and incorporate what you hear.

Crafting a strong personal brand starts with understanding yourself (yes – the good, the bad and the ugly) and building upon your strengths and the things that make you shine.

ASSESS YOUR CURRENT BRAND

The first step is an assessment. What is your current personal brand? What elements work in your favor and which ones work against you?

Even if you haven't proactively thought about your personal brand yet, people already have perceptions about you. You're also likely already building a presence online, even if it is shared with only those you choose.

Start by taking some time to learn more about how others perceive you. Ask yourself and, ideally, others, the following questions:

- What are the top words that people use to describe me, personally?
- What are the top words people use to describe me professionally?
- What are the top words my boss (or a former boss) would use to describe me?
- How do I benefit the people I work with?
- How do I make people feel?
- When I meet a new person, what do they remember about me?

Try to be as honest as possible as you answer these questions. It will give you an idea of your current brand but also some of your strengths that you can use and build on as you start determining how to position yourself.

Action Item

Ask your close coworkers, friends, and clients to write a short five sentence bio about you, as though they were introducing you as a professional speaker, or as a winner of an award. Take note of what they say and how they position you. What do you like? What would you change?

Test Your Current Brand

Another tip to test your current brand (or the brand that you create) is to see what people remember when you actually meet them in person.

Attend a networking event, or another event where you will meet other professionals. Introduce yourself to someone new and spend a few minutes chatting with the person. Next excuse yourself from the conversation.

Wait five minutes and have a friend start a conversation with the same person you just met. Have them ask the new person about you "Hey, I noticed you were speaking to Krista earlier, what does she do?"

Take note of what they remember and how accurately they can share who you are and what you do. This helps you understand if your brand message is memorable. Do this over and over again as you grow and evolve your brand to test the effectiveness.

Power Tip:
The best way to evaluate the strength of any aspect of your personal brand is to see if someone else can understand and repeat it back to you. If they don't understand or can't remember, you need to keep working.

EXPLORE YOURSELF

After evaluating your current personal brand, it can be helpful to explore yourself. The above step focused on how other people perceive you, but it is also important to think about yourself – your passions, values, strengths, personality traits, and personal aspects that you want to incorporate into your brand.

Think about:

- What are your top professional skills?
- What are your biggest strengths?
- What are your top personal attributes?
- What is your personality type?
- What role do you typically enjoy being in on a team?
- What do you love to do?
- What are your values?

Tools
It can be helpful to use some guided tools to learn more about yourself. Check out the Strengths Finder at **https://high5test.com/test/** and the Myers Briggs personality test at **http://www.humanmetrics.com/cgi-win/jtypes2.asp**

GET INSPIRED

As you embark on this journey it is helpful to have some people to reference who you admire or can learn from. While not every personal brand will match how you want to portray yourself, you can learn something from every execution.

For example, Gary Vaynerchuck has built a strong and powerful (and profitable) personal brand for himself. While my personality and style are different than his, I have learned a lot by observing how he lets his personality shine through and uses video to tell his story.

Look for people with personal brands that you can learn from – whether it is their style, their positioning, their execution, or their approach. It can also be helpful to see things that won't work for you – for example when I see overly promotional personal brands, I am reminded to balance my promotion with my content better.

To find some people that you can look to for inspiration, do some searching on Google, LinkedIn, and other social networks:

- Thought leaders in your industry
- People doing what you want to do
- Top personal branders
- Industry experts you follow on LinkedIn
- Celebrities or personalities that match the persona you want to radiate

As you look at others, consider what you like and don't like about what they do.

Action Item

Find 5–10 people that you think do a good job with their personal brand that you can learn from. Make a list of them and also write down what you like and don't like about their execution.

EVALUATE YOUR CURRENT BRAND

> ➤ What is the current perception that people have about you?
> ➤ What are your best strengths and skills – professionally and personally?
> ➤ Who are 5–10 people that you can look to and learn from as you develop your brand?

_____

_____

_____

_____

_____

What is the big thing you want to remember from this chapter?

_____

_____

Go to www.LaunchYourself.com/book for your free action planner and bonus resources.

PART 2: DEFINE YOUR PERSONAL BRAND

The first step in building a powerful personal brand is to step back and define your brand. Why are you embarking on this, what do you want to achieve, and what is your starting point?

The biggest mistake people and businesses make when it comes to creating an online presence is that they start with the tools without a clear vision of the "what" and "why." Investing upfront in defining your personal brand will make it easier to bring it to life online in a meaningful and impactful way.

Remember – you may not have perfect answer to every question in this stage. Get as close as possible and move on. You can revisit and refine this over time.

CHAPTER 5: YOUR WHY – DEFINE YOUR OBJECTIVES AND AUDIENCE

Before you even get started defining your personal brand, it can be helpful to explore your personal goals and objectives. Why are you creating a personal brand? What do you want it to do for you?

When it comes to personal branding there are many different directions that you can take. Knowing **why** you want to create a personal brand will bring clarity to your efforts and help you maintain focus.

When you have a clear idea of your objectives and the type of opportunities you want to attract, you increase the likelihood that your personal brand will, indeed, attract them.

Big Idea
The more you know about what you want, the more likely you are to get it. Knowing what you want will help you craft a brand that attracts the results you want.

Krista Neher

YOUR OBJECTIVES

Why are you creating a personal brand? What do you want it to achieve for you?

This could be an easy or more challenging question for you to answer for yourself depending on where you are in your career.

What do you want for yourself and your career over the next 2-5 years?

- More clients?
- Better opportunities?
- A larger network?
- A promotion?
- New job opportunities?
- To grow sales?
- To build your public reputation?
- To be seen as an expert?
- To start a business?
- To promote a product?

What about in 10 years?

Thinking about your short- and long-term goals will help you uncover why you are creating a brand for yourself.

What are some things that you want to get from your personal brand?

In addition to your general or broad career goals, there may be specific opportunities that you would like to get from your brand. A well-crafted brand will attract the opportunities you want – so consider some specific things you want for yourself in the future.

This could include:

- Book deals
- Speaking
- Clients
- Sales
- Job offers
- Become a coach
- Expert opportunities
- Press opportunities
- A promotion at work
- Improved perception at work
- Career change
- Start a business
- Become industry leader
- Become an influencer
- Earn Board positions
- Get a teaching position
- Become a consultant
- Sell a product
- Share your knowledge
- Promote/advocate for your company
- Run for political office
- Share your passions
- Build a business
- Get published in industry publications
- Get funding for a startup
- Manage your reputation in a public position
- Achieve recognition at work

YOUR TARGET AUDIENCE

Defining the audience you want your brand to reach is important, as you may make different choices depending on your desired target.

For example, Dr. Phil, a famous television psychologist is trying to reach averages Americans. He has created a brand that is clear, approachable, and "tells it like it is." He speaks about things in an easy-to-understand way while at the same time maintaining his knowledge and expertise. Imagine if Dr. Phil wanted to reach doctors instead. He would probably choose a different style and alter almost every aspect of his personal brand.

Big Idea
Know who you want to reach with your personal brand and think about what they will respond to. It may be different than other audiences.

Defining your target audience will help you make better choices about your personal branding execution.

Based on your objectives, who is your target audience? You may have more than one, but the fewer and more specific they are the better.

Who is your target audience?

- Clients
- Prospects
- Superiors at work
- Industry though-leaders
- The target of your business/product
- Media

- People in a specific role/industry

When I started building my personal brand, I wanted to position myself as a social media expert, and my target audience was "marketing people." My objective wasn't clear, neither was my target audience. When I choose a clear objective of gaining paid speaking engagements I focused in on meeting and event planners and was able to create a clear social media plan for myself using only two channels. By having a clear idea of my goal and my target audience I went from a broad idea about my personal brand to a clear and specific focus that generated results - three paid engagements in three months!

DEFINE YOUR OBJECTIVE AND TARGET AUDIENCE

➢ What is your objective for building your personal brand?

➢ What are some specific things that you want your brand to deliver for you?

➢ Who is the target audience that you need to reach to achieve?

_____

_____

_____

_____

_____

_____

What is the big thing you want to remember from this chapter?

_____

_____

Go to www.LaunchYourself.com/book for your free action planner and bonus resources.

CHAPTER 6: DEFINE YOURSELF PROFESSIONALLY AND PERSONALLY

The key to creating a compelling brand that attracts opportunities is to deliberately and specifically define the brand that you want to create. In this chapter we'll focus on exploring and defining the professional and personal aspects of your personal brand that you want to feature. At the end of this chapter we'll synthesize your definition down into your personal brand statement.

As you seek to define yourself, keep in mind that authenticity is a key component of an effective personal brand. Your brand should build off of your strengths and be natural to you. A brand built on a persona that doesn't match who you really are will be difficult to maintain and probably won't connect with people. Your brand should feel natural to you.

Your brand also needs to connect with both the hearts and minds of the people that you want to reach. Brands are both logical and emotional. This is why strategically incorporating your personality and personal interests into your brand is important. People want to get to know YOU – and you are a person beyond your professional presence.

A big part of connecting with people, and a core principle of influence, is that we work with people we know, like, and trust. When it comes to likability, it's based on similarities, empathy, or understanding of others and getting to know people. If your brand is too professional, you miss the opportunity to really connect with them on an emotional and real level.

While you certainly don't want to share every detail of your personal life, and different people have different approaches on what they share about family, hobbies, and politics or other personal matters, finding aspects of your personal life that you are comfortable sharing is key if you really want to connect.

In this chapter we'll explore and define the key content and attributes of your professional life, your personal life, and your personality that you want to build your personal brand on.

DEFINE YOURSELF PROFESSIONALLY

Your professional definition helps you to brainstorm and evaluate your professional strengths and positioning. While there are probably many people that do what you do, there is nobody who does it like you.

The goal is to define yourself professionally in a way that sets you apart from your peers, highlights your skills and accomplishments, and puts you in the position of being the best.

We sometimes don't do a great job at seeing what is truly remarkable about ourselves. When I started to build my personal brand and speaking at conferences, attendees asked me what I did and I would just unassumingly say "social media." At one conference after I gave my typical answers, a friend chimed in "Krista is being modest. She was an executive at P&G and was one of the first social media marketers – even marketing on Myspace. She now runs a really successful training company." I had never thought to mention these things when I introduced myself. I also did a terrible job at stating what I did.

I realized that I couldn't rely on my friends jumping in to represent me well –
I needed to explore the things that made me credible and gain confidence
mentioning them when I met people.

In defining your professional self, regardless of where you are in your career,
is to think about what you do and how to explain it to others.

- What field or industry are you in or do you want to be in?
- What are the words used to describe your work or industry?
- How can you more specifically define your talents into a niche?
- Can you be more specific about what you do – for example a lawyer
  vs. a trial lawyer who specializes in civil disputes with a strength in
  jury assessment.
- What are the core skills for what you do?
- How do you do your job better/differently than others in your
  profession?
- What sets you apart from others who do what you do?
- What are your greatest professional strengths?
- What are you best at?
- What do you love the most about your job or what you do? (This
  could be functional – solving complex problems – or emotional –
  helping people.)
- What experiences do you have that make you stand out? (experience,
  clients, courses, programs, employers, education)

The above questions will help you to think about your professional strengths
to bring to life in your personal brand. You may not have answers to every
question right now – **that is okay.**

I still don't have the perfect answers to all of the personal branding
questions. Spend some time thinking about each question and generating
your best response and then move forward.

Remember:
Others may see you better than you can see yourself. Don't hesitate to ask trusted friends and coworkers. Many of the best parts of my personal brand came from me listening to what other people said about me.

DEFINE YOUR PERSONALITY

Defining your personality is about focusing on the areas of it that you want to bring across with your personal brand. What aspects are best matched with your personal brand? Which ones should you let shine?

Personality is really important. Think back to the example of Dr. Phil. He probably isn't the smartest, best or most knowledgeable psychologist, but he is one of the most followed. It isn't because of his knowledge. It's because of his big personality – he is straightforward and makes things easy for people to understand. His no BS style attracts people to him.

Remember:
Your personal brand connects with the hearts and minds of your target audience, and your personality is a big part of this! Personality will build stronger connections with people than any amount of professional knowledge or expertise.

It may be helpful to also re-examine some of the other personal brands you reviewed earlier to evaluate the elements of personality that shine through and inspire you. People connect with people – so getting your personality across is key.

Power Tip:
Sometimes we take ourselves for granted or fail to see the parts that other people really appreciate. Check back with

friends and family to gain some insights on the parts of your personality that really connect with people.

Evaluate your personality to choose the elements that you want to incorporate into your personal brand.

- What is most memorable about you? When people meet you, the thing that they remember is _____ (this could be personality, physical, trait, behavior, etc.)
- People like to work with me because:
- My friends would say that my personality is:
- The aspects of my personality that I want my brand to portray are:

DEFINE YOURSELF PERSONALLY

People connect with PEOPLE and building connections with people involves exposing parts of your personal and professional life. One of the best ways to connect with people is through commonalities – which often link back to our personal interests or hobbies. These can also be memorable and set you apart from others.

This is why résumés often include a section for hobbies and interests – because this creates connections and helps potential employers to get to know you.

Power Tip:
If you have personal interests or interesting things that you can share about yourself this can actually be more memorable and build a deeper connection than all of your professional accomplishments. While we focus a lot on credibility and professionalism, the things that people often remember about you are personal – even in a professional context.

The most successful personal brands reveal and share parts of their personal lives based on the image they are trying to craft. Consider what makes you interesting beyond your work to make your brand more relatable and compelling.

- What are your passions? These can be both personal and professional. If you had nothing else to motivate you, what would you get out of bed at 5:00 AM every day?
- What are your personal values? For example: Balance, being the best, agility, calmness, challenge, decisiveness, perseverance, drive, honesty, integrity, pragmatism, sensitivity, structure, teamwork, sharing, vitality, zeal.
- What are your hobbies? What do you like to do in your free time?
- What interesting things have you done or accomplished personally? What are you most proud of?
- What parts of your personal life are off-limits, or do you not plan to share?

CRAFTING YOUR DESCRIPTIONS

After examining your professional, personal, and personality strengths and differences the next step is to bring it together into your professional description, solution, benefit, and USP. These elements will make up your Personal Brand Statement which is the roadmap you'll use to bring your personal brand to life.

Your Professional Description

This is how you explain to people what you do. While this may seem easy, many people get it wrong. They are often too vague (for example when I said I did "social media") or they are complicated, so people don't understand what they actually do, for example "I provide disposal system engineering to maximize waste removal."

Your professional description should be clear, simple, and easy for someone to understand. If someone can't understand what you do, they can't introduce you to other people or bring you opportunities.

Power Tip:
The best brands and professional opportunities are easy to remember and share. If someone can't easily understand what you do, they can't connect you with opportunities or tell other people about you. This should be your test as to if your brand is clear and simple enough.

Even if your target audience in your industry would understand a more technical professional description, you want your personal brand to have the ability to travel by word-of-mouth. Many of the people you meet will be outside of your field and not understand a technical description. It may be helpful to have two professional descriptions if you work in a highly technical or specialized field – one for those in your industry and one for the general public. This will allow you to communicate effectively to both groups.

While your professional description should be clear and simple, it also must be specific. What exactly do you do? Not "insurance" but "I am an insurance broker specializing in personal coverage." Not "social media" but "digital marketing trainer for business."

- I'm an insurance broker.
- I'm a digital marketing trainer.
- I'm a business consultant.

Action Item:
Craft your professional description to describe what you do as clearly as possible. Remember that it should be easily understood by average people and your target audience.

What do you do? _____.

(professional description – clear, simple, no jargon, easy to understand)

Professional Solution

Your professional solution is the solution that you provide. What does someone get when they work with you? This can be specific and should hone in on a part of what makes you stand out vs. others in your field.

For example, Rachael Ray and Martha Stewart will both give me recipes (professional description), but the solution is very different. Rachael Ray gives me delicious and practical solutions for my family. Martha Stewart gives me impressive meals for entertaining friends.

Your solution should focus on what someone gets from working with you as specifically as possible. This is where you can really set yourself apart with a more compelling solution. Sample solutions would be:

- I help people sell their home quickly.
- I help people understand digital marketing.
- I help people find ways to grow their business.

Even within one industry there can be countless solutions depending on your point of difference. For example, consider a real estate agent. Their solution could be:

- I sell homes quickly.
- I make selling your house fun.
- I get you the most $$$ for your home.
- Selling your home has never been so easy.

This list could go on and on. The idea is that even when the result is the same (a sold house) the solution (the way you get to the sold house) could be different. This is what typically sets you apart from others in your industry.

Action Item:
Craft your professional solution to describe what people get from working with you. Think beyond the function to the differentiator that you provide.

What is the solution that you provide? _____.

(professional solution – how do you help people, what do they get, logical + emotional)

47

Professional Benefit

The benefit is what they get from your solution. Why do they care about your solution? How does it benefit them? The professional benefit is the "hook" to what you do – it focuses on the audience and what is in it for them.

Your professional benefit should focus on results and it can be functional or emotional.

Take a product like whitening toothpaste. The solution is that it makes your teeth whiter, but the benefit is more confidence, looking your best on the big day, being more attractive, etc. Most product and service marketing focuses on the benefit instead because this is what really drives people to make a decision. Some people may think that the benefit is the whiter teeth, but that is simply the solution. The benefit is much deeper.

If we go back to our real estate example, each professional solution provides different benefits. For example:

- I sell homes quickly
  - So you have less stress
  - So you can get into your dream home quicker
  - To minimize disruptions in your life
  - So you have less uncertainty

As you can see, even with one solution there could be a few different benefits. It is helpful to think in terms of your target audience to understand what professional benefits are most important to them.

 Power Tip:
To get to an impactful benefit it is often helpful to brainstorm the different benefits that your solution generates and choose the one or two that are most meaningful.

Try to make your benefit as specific as possible and make sure that it is a reasonable outcome of your solution. For example, if I said I provide digital marketing training to help people live their dream life, that might be a bit of a stretch. "Better results faster" is more specific and related to my solution.

Action Item:
Craft your professional benefit that describes the benefit(s) that people get from your solution. Try to limit yourself to 1-2 so as to stay focused.

What is the benefit from what you do? _____.

(professional benefit – what is the benefit that someone gets, what is unique about you)

Unique Selling Proposing (USP)

Your professional solution and benefit have probably already started to differentiate you vs. others in your field. Your USP is how you specifically stake your claim on how you are different than others.

Brands do this in order to stand out in a crowded market place. If you think of laundry detergent (an area where I used to do marketing) Tide is the market leader and the best clean, Gain has the best and freshest scents, Purex is good value, Cheer is the best for protecting clothes. All laundry detergent essentially does the same thing – cleans clothes – but each brand has a unique proposition to the consumer.

What makes you unique at what you do? Brainstorm ideas and circle the one or two that you want to focus on.

- What do you do better or faster?

- What makes you better to work with vs someone else?
- How do you approach your work differently?
- Are there parts of your personality that set you apart?
- Do you have credibility or specialization that makes you unique?

Your unique selling proposition should highlight what makes you stand out. This is challenging for most business professionals to define. What is it that makes you unique? This could be skill related such as data-driven marketing, personality related such as easy to work with, or specialization focused such as the biggest law firm marketing company.

- Professional proof points – Bestselling author
- Approach – Passionate about customers
- Process – Use a 4 Stage System for groups
- Personality – Never have more fun planning your financial future!

If you are having trouble with your USP think about how you approach things differently to drive results for your clients or business partners.

 Action Item:
Craft your USP. If you struggle to find something get as close as you can for now and keep moving forward with the process. This can be one of the more difficult parts.

What is your unique selling proposition? _____.

(USP – what do you do that is different/better vs. others).

CRAFTING YOUR PERSONAL BRAND STATEMENT

All of the above elements come together into your Personal Brand Statement.

I am a (professional description) digital marketing speaker and trainer **who is (personality and USP)** passionate, entertaining, and inspirational; a bestselling author and global speaker **who helps people (professional solution)** understand what actually works in digital marketing **so that (professional benefit)** they can get better results faster.

Remember:
Keep in mind that you will use this to build the rest of your brand – but it doesn't have to be perfectly worded or ready to engrave on a trophy. This is your guiding roadmap for how you bring your personal brand to life. You can always come back and change it as you grow and evolve.

Your
Personal Brand
Statement

My goal from my personal brand is:

_____

_____

I am (professional description)

_____

_____

Who is (personality)

_____

_____

And helps people (professional solution)

_____

_____

So that (professional benefit)

_____

_____

Sample Personal Brand Statement:

My goal is to earn speaking and training clients by being seen as an expert in my field. My target audience is marketers and digital marketers. **I am** a digital marketing speaker and traininer **who is** passionate, entertaining and inspirational **and helps people** understand digital marketing **so that** they can get better results faster.

DEFINE YOURSELF AND CRAFT YOUR PERSONAL BRAND STATEMENT

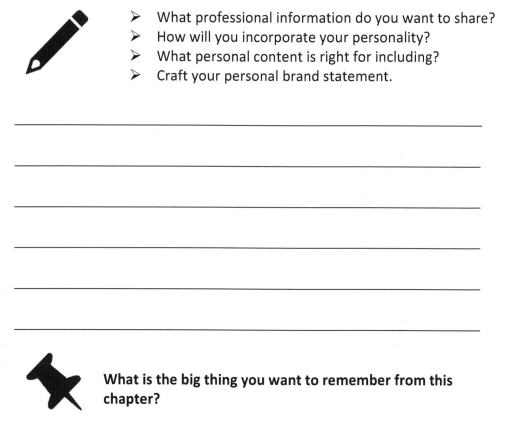

➢ What professional information do you want to share?
➢ How will you incorporate your personality?
➢ What personal content is right for including?
➢ Craft your personal brand statement.

_____

_____

_____

_____

_____

_____

What is the big thing you want to remember from this chapter?

_____

_____

Go to www.LaunchYourself.com/book for your free action planner and bonus resources.

PART 3: DESIGNING YOUR PERSONAL BRAND

Now that you know **what** you want to communicate with your personal brand (your Personal Brand Statement) it is time to determine **how** to communicate it. Regardless of how strong your personal brand statement is, if you don't communicate it effectively it won't make an impact.

Designing your personal brand focuses on crafting something that is compelling and desirable.

This section is based on the branding principles that have created some of the most powerful and iconic brands in the world – from Harley Davidson to Apple Computers to Pampers to Old Spice.

We'll focus on creating your personal branding pyramid:

- Building Blocks: This is the foundation of your personal brand and focuses on the elements to highlight to make yourself memorable, authentic, distinctive, and educated.
- Brand Character: What is the style, look, feel, values, personality, and tone of your brand?
- Mission: Crafting a mission-based statement that embodies what you do and why you do it.
- Design Elements: The visuals you use to bring your brand to life.

Your
Personal Brand
Pyramid

Mission

What are you
all about?

Brand Character

How do you come across
personally?

Your personality, style & values.

Building Blocks

An emotional connection –
How do you draw people in?

*The things that make you: Memorable,
Authentic, Different, Educated.*

Design Elements

How do you bring your brand
to life?

Both online & in-person.

CHAPTER 7: DESIGNING YOUR BUILDING BLOCKS

Your building blocks are the foundational elements of your personal brand. They are where you define what you want to communicate.

The elements that create strong building blocks are summarized as MADE: Memorable, Authentic, Different, and Educated.

These elements serve two purposes. First the MADE elements should help you to identify the things that you want to get across with your personal brand. As you execute it, you want to incorporate elements of each MADE category to craft a desirable brand that attracts the opportunities you want.

Second, as you embark on bringing your brand to life, these principles will strengthen your execution. Whether you execute your personal brand online or in person, the MADE elements should guide your choices to be sure you are crafting a memorable brand that connects with people and positions you uniquely and credibly.

These building blocks are based on hundreds of years of branding research about what makes strong brands and adapted for personal branding.

4 Elements of a
WOW! Brand

Memorable

Will people remember you after they meet you? Is your brand singular and simple?

SPECIFIC • SIMPLE • CONSISTENT

Authentic

Does your brand match who you really are, and come across as genuine?

REAL • STRENGTHS-BASED • PERSONALITY

Different

Is your brand specific and unique?
Do you stand out?

UNIQUE • POINT OF DIFFERENCE • SPECIALIZATION

Educated

Is your brand credible and believable based on your actual background, achievements, etc.?

EXPERIENCE • CREDIBILITY • ACCOMPLISHMENTS

MEMORABLE

Memorability is one of the most important aspects of a personal brand. If people can't remember you or your brand it will be difficult to make an impact. Some people think about crafting a memorable personal brand as focusing on appearance, or a trademark look, color, or accessory, but it's actually much deeper than that. Memorability is about crafting every aspect of your brand in a way that people are likely to recall it.

Some of the elements of memorability have been touched on in the define stage; the three key elements to a memorable brand are being specific, simple, and consistent.

Specificity

When I started building my personal brand, I didn't want to pigeon-hole myself as a social media marketer – after all, I had spent years doing strategic brand marketing and only a year in social media. At the time (2006/2007) social media was emerging as a real business tool, and there weren't many marketers who specialized in it. I was focusing on social media, but I felt that I could do so much more. So, when people asked what I did, I'd give a list: strategic marketing, social media, branding, blah, blah, blah.

In an effort to "not miss out" I created a broad definition of my brand. The problem was that this wasn't sticky or memorable. If someone asked "What does Krista do?" the answer probably would have been "something with marketing." Nobody needs "something with marketing"!!! It isn't desirable or memorable because it is too broad. When I said "social media" (and this was in the early days of social media before so many people did it) I got referrals and clients.

59

If you have to say "and" in your definition of what you do you aren't being specific enough. You are lucky if people remember one clear thing – they won't remember many. Focus on the one thing that is most likely to attract the opportunities you want.

Power Tip:
This story also highlights another point, which is that your brand will (and should) evolve as the landscape changes. When social media was niche, being "the social media person" was specific enough. As social media grew, I needed to get more specific. Pay attention to changes in how people respond to your brand and the market and use that to guide your choices.

Simplicity

Keep your brand as simple and clear as possible. Studies show that people need to see an advertisement seven (7!!) times before they even remember it. If you try to communicate too much you will end up communicating nothing at all. This is good to remember as a general principle.

Less is more.

Keep all elements of your brand as clear and simple as possible.

A number of years ago I met a guy at an industry event focused on Search Engine Optimization, which is about getting to the top of Google search results. I wanted to get in touch with him after the event but I'm terrible with names. Then I remembered that he told me he was The Coolest Guy in Kansas City. Seriously – if you google it, he shows up. I couldn't remember his name, but I remembered this simple story that he told me. The interesting thing about being The Coolest Guy in Kansas City (which is ironic since he is somewhat nerdy) is that it also shows his credibility as an SEO expert since he got his personal website to the top of Google for this search.

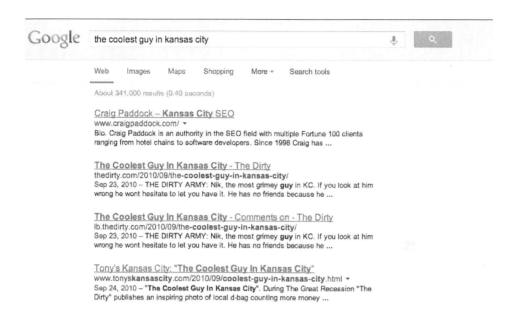

Many years ago, I was giving a presentation on social media, and someone asked if everyone was really on Facebook. My dad had just joined, so I showed them his profile. In addition to proving that even an almost 70-year old man with dial-up internet was on Facebook, everyone was quite amused to learn that my father is an Elvis enthusiast and tribute artist.

I started incorporating my Elvis-dad into some of my talks – not just to publicly mock him but to make a point about positioning. Side note - why does he want to be positioned as an Elvis when he is on city council?? One day I got a call from a prospective client inviting me to do a keynote presentation. She told me that years ago she joined a webinar and was literally laughing out loud about my father being an Elvis. She remembered me for years because of my Elvis dad (thank you, Dad, if you are reading this). The point isn't to further publicly discuss my Elvis dad, it is to show that sometimes the simplest things can be very memorable.

Pay attention to what people remember and try to build off of it. It is often the simple things that are memorable. Sometimes they are the personal things you share.

Consistency

From an executional standpoint, consistency is important to build a strong brand image. This is why doing the define and design work upfront is helpful – if you have a clear idea of the impression that you want to create, you can deliver it consistently over time.

Brands know this – this is why their logo always looks the same and they show it in all of their marketing. They are also consistent about their marketing messages, brand positioning, and benefits. The reason consistency is important is because most people don't remember everything they see. In order to be remembered, the brand must look similar to drive an impression.

Personal brands also need to be consistent to be memorable and create impact. This means that all elements of your brand should be delivered as consistently as possible over time. The similarity each time you interact with someone makes you more memorable.

When I started out in speaking and building my brand, I would sometimes where my hair up and other times keep it down. What I realized is that as small of a detail a hairstyle might be, people who saw me with my hair up didn't recognize me with my hair down. I started to keep my hair up for all professional events to make my visual image as consistent as possible. It made a huge difference. Even at large networking events people could easily spot me in a crowd and people would "recognize" me from Twitter or LinkedIn because I looked consistent and presented myself similarly on each platform.

A quick Google Image search of Martha Stewart shows how visually consistent her look is (except in some news shots she can't control). Consistency breeds familiarity and memorability.

This principle applies well beyond physical or visible attributes. The way you present yourself, what you do, and your benefits should be consistently presented to maximize the memorability and impact.

Power Tip:
Build a professional brand that you can execute consistency to build memorability and solidify your positioning in people's minds.

Action:
Make note of the things that make you memorable – specific, simple, and consistent. Consider what people already remember about you and build on it.

AUTHENTIC

A personal brand should be personal – which means it should be authentic. Have you ever talked to someone and they just seemed really fake? You felt like they were putting on an act? This happens when we try to be something we aren't. Establishing a strong personal brand means being confident in who you are and authentic to yourself.

Even for the same objectives and target audiences, different brand styles can work for different people. The key is to build a connection with your audience which happens when you connect with them in an authentic way.

Authenticity comes from three things: being real, focusing on your strengths, and showcasing your personality and personal side in an appropriate way.

Real

Being real is about being authentic and natural to yourself. Trying to be something you aren't will put up a wall and make it difficult for people to connect with you and connection is a key part of your personal brand success.

The reason that this book starts with personal reflection and discovery is so that you can dive deeper into who you really are and what you bring to the table so that you can bring it to life in a meaningful way with your personal brand.

Be real. Be human.

Don't be afraid to reveal things (strategically of course) that are less than perfect about yourself. Many speakers start with self-deprecating humor as a way to be more relatable. They share a story about how they failed or made a big mistake. This is because the failure makes them relatable and draws people in.

One popular online marketing blogger who was a leading authority with a massive following for his online marketing advice had a section on his website called "I used to be fat." He had lost tons of weight and shared his story, as well as before and after pictures. This was the single most popular section of his website. People loved to hear his real story and it made him relatable.

When I started my personal blog, I wrote a blog post about my New Year's resolutions, which included learning guitar. Most of my content was about marketing, but I wanted to ring in the New Year with something a little more personal. What surprised me was in five different meetings in January, business contacts asked about how my guitar lessons were going. I got more feedback (both online and offline) about an honest and personal post than I did for most of my business content. People like to connect with people and sharing real content about yourself strengthens relationships.

In building your brand you may be inclined to make things sound perfect and polished, but actually, people will also connect with you if you can be relatable and real.

As you build your personal brand, make sure that it is true to who you really are, and avoid the risk of getting so buttoned up and professional that people don't feel that you are real.

Power Tip:
Pay attention to things that you share about yourself that people respond positively to. Consider incorporating these into your brand. For example, as a Canadian I often open with a comment about being nicer than Americans as a way to share something that builds connection with people.

Strengths-Based Focus

Your personal brand should focus on showcasing and capitalizing on your strengths. In order to do this effectively you have to understand what your strengths are.

In Part 1: Defining your Personal Brand we focused on exploring yourself to better understand where your strengths really lie. An authentic brand focuses on bringing your unique strengths to life.

Remember:
For most of us it is difficult to see our strengths and feel comfortable capitalizing on them. If you aren't sure, ask your friends or coworkers for help.

Personality Driven

The strongest personal brands are seeping with personality. You feel like you are really getting to know the person. In building an authentic brand that connects with people you need to let your personality shine through.

When building a personal brand many business professionals feel that they need to focus only on the professional. This couldn't be further from the truth! Credibility is only one of the four characteristics of a strong brand.

Your personality is what sets you apart and drives people to you.

It can be hard to put yourself out there but for everyone who doesn't like you many, many, many more will LOVE you. When I deliver presentations, I often receive extremely high feedback – I'll get mostly 5/5 but there may also be a few 2s or 3s. If you don't let your real self come through, you'll get stuck in the 3 – 4 range. People won't hate you, but they won't love you.

Gary Vaynerchuck is a great (albeit extreme) example of bringing personality into your personal brand. Although he is a business expert, he uses foul language, speaks off the cuff, and spouts out opinions about everything. Yet he has a huge following and is regularly invited to deliver keynote presentations for large Fortune 500 companies.

Power Tip:
Think about a handful of personality traits that you want to bring through in your personal brand. Be deliberate in the personality that you craft for yourself and execute it consistently to drive impact.

Action:
Consider how to build a brand that connects with people by bring your authenticity in to your execution – Real, Strengths-based, and Personality Driven.

DIFFERENT

Uniqueness or distinctiveness is a key attribute of a powerful brand. Regardless of your space, there are lots of people who do what you do. This is where you stand out and set yourself apart vs. your peers. This is why people choose you vs. someone else. Difference is comprised of three elements: uniqueness, points of difference, and specialization.

Difference is really about how you position your brand relative to other people. The strongest brands have clear and distinctive positioning. For example, the ice cream section in a supermarket has lots of different positioning. Some are based on indulgence (Haagen-Dazs), others on price (store brand), a few on health (Skinny Cow), another on natural ingredients (Breyer's natural line), and some on taste and ingredients (Ben and Jerry's). There are also tons of smaller brands that usually each have a specialized value proposition.

Brands (and personal brands) that are more differentiated can often demand a premium price as well. The more unique your brand is the fewer alternatives there are. By making yourself distinctive you may appeal to fewer people, but you will have a stronger value proposition to the people that you appeal to.

When I started in social media it wasn't a crowded space – I was one of the first social media marketers. In a few years it seemed that there were millions of them, so I needed to further differentiate myself. I did this in two ways.

First, I became more specialized. Rather than just being a "social media marketer" I became a social media trainer. So, I specialized further to differentiate myself.

Second, I focused on my credibility builders. Sure, lots of people were now social media marketers, but I was a pioneer in social media, creating one of the first business Twitter accounts. My overall brand positioning became focused around "the real deal in social media" to differentiate myself from those less experienced.

Differentiating yourself requires looking at others in your space and determining how you will stand out from them.

Uniqueness

u·nique

/yōo'nēk/ ◄》

adjective

1. being the only one of its kind; unlike anything else.
"the situation was unique in modern politics"

When we are kids, we are told that we are special and different than anyone else. As adults we lose this sense as our logical brains kick in and we struggle to see objectively what makes us different.

The truth is that we are all unique. The challenge is remembering why.

Your uniqueness could come from your story, your background, your qualifications, your skills, your personality, your personal passions, your energy, your values, how you deliver your services, or how you approach your job.

This is an area that I really struggled to define for myself. I have a lot of qualifications and accomplishments in my résumé, which definitely position me differently, but what I think really makes me unique is my style of delivery. In speaking, my energy, passion, and enthusiasm are contagious and inspirational (or at least that is my hope) and the same is true when working with clients. I want to leave them inspired and excited. That is what makes me unique. Not only do I help them to get better results from digital marketing, I inspire them to get excited about it and believe that they can do it. This point of uniqueness for me is a little aspirational – I'm not sure that this is delivered 100% of the time, but this is what I aim for with my personal brand.

What are some of the things that make you unique or different vs. others in your industry? What can you highlight to be more distinctive?

Point of Difference

When you think about the competitive edge of a business it is usually focused on providing a specific and meaningful point of difference vs. their competitors. For example, Jiffy Lube focuses on their point of difference being speed. It doesn't mean that they have bad quality, but speed of service is what sets them apart from their competition.

For personal brands you need a similar point of difference. What is the **one thing** that is meaningful to your audience that sets you apart from other people.

My point of difference is in my credibility and experience – when it comes to speaking, training, and digital marketing you would be hard pressed to find someone with more credentials and experience than me.

This may be challenging to determine. Most businesses struggle to find this which weakens their positioning (and sales) in the marketplace.

Think about your personal brand. What makes you or your offering different from others? This could be experience, qualifications, approach, personality, etc. Why would I choose you over someone else?

Specialization

One strategy to differentiate yourself is through specializations. Specializing means defining the scope of what you do more narrowly. Instead of being a coach, be a coach for busy moms focused on balance.

From a business strategy standpoint, niche businesses tend to be more effective vs. broad businesses, yet as individuals we often fail to define ourselves specifically. We want to highlight everything we can do instead of focusing on what we really do best.

A friend of mine, Mark Homer, started a business called Get Noticed Get Found focusing on digital marketing for law firms. Their knowledge and services could work well in almost any industry, so why limit themselves by just working with lawyers? Because they could be the best and only online marketing for lawyers. They built a big and sustainable business by focusing on a specialized area. Sure, they turn down business from non-lawyers, but they are able to be the best at servicing lawyers, build a strong brand, and charge a premium.

If you needed a photographer for your wedding, would you rather hire and pay more for someone who specialized in weddings and could give you a detailed wedding plan or a photographer who could also shoot your business product photography, headshots, pets, concerts, and stock photography?

Consider specializing to be different. For example, there are hundreds of thousands of social media managers, but only a few specializing in restaurants. How can you specialize yourself to be "the best" at something specific?

Action:
In order for your brand to stand out it must be distinctive. What are the things that make you unique, what is a point-of-difference that you can highlight, and how can you specialize to be the best?

EDUCATED

This element focuses on your credibility – why would someone believe that you are what you say you are? Why should they buy into your personal brand?

You'll want to get these elements across to people to validate your personal brand and come across as believable. For example, if I am the best at social media for restaurants, what are some proof points I have that demonstrate this? What experience, credibility boosters, or accomplishments make this believable?

Depending on where you are in your professional journey, this may be easy or challenging, and sometimes takes creative positioning. For example, at the beginning of my personal branding journey a friend described me as a "Former P&G executive who was a pioneer in social media." I would never in a million years thought to position myself that way. "Executive" was a liberal definition of my role and I hadn't thought of myself as a "pioneer" even though it was all true. He took parts of my résumé and positioned them in a way that made me sound amazing!

Example:
A friend of mine needed to submit his bio for an award he won, and it initially read "Person X is an animator and designer with over 10 years of experience." After exploring his credibility, we updated it to "Person X is an award-winning animator and designer having created visual effects for

> Hollywood movies, designed television commercials for Target, Pampers, and Lens Crafters, concepted three television cartoons, and taught others as a professor for over 10 years."

If you are struggling with this section, you may need to be creative (but never dishonest) in your positioning. You may also come up with some goals for yourself to grow your credibility. When I got started, I wanted to have a "as seen on" section on my site showing off media appearances like other professional speakers had. So, I set this as a goal and started actively looking for local media opportunities. My local news stations were CBS, NBC, and Fox affiliates, so getting on their segments would allow me to include their coverage on my site. It took a few years, but I gained 4–5 recognized media appearances.

Remember:
As you go through this process, you may also think about things you'd like to be able to add to your list. Keep note of these and you can add them to the goals of your personal brand. For example, if I wanted to add "award winning" I could seek out award opportunities and craft entries.

Start with what you have and then think about positioning or framing it. Don't be afraid to set goals for yourself if you want to grow your credibility further. This section may give you some ideas of goals to set for yourself.

If you are early in your career you may not have a lot yet. Don't let this deter you! Consider how to position what you have done to make the most out of your existing experience.

Experience

Experience focuses on your background and the work that you have done that is relevant to your brand positioning.

Depending on if you are trying to reposition your brand, you may choose to reposition some of your experiences. For example, a number of years ago I was asked to review a LinkedIn profile for a social media position. There was no evidence of social media anywhere on the LinkedIn profile. A few days later a colleague sent me the résumé of the same person and it was loaded with social media experience. It wasn't that the résumé or LinkedIn profile was dishonest or untrue, it was that the experience highlighted different things based on the objectives.

As a side note this is why consistency is so important. Her credibility was immediately questionable by seeing two totally different views of her experience.

What relevant experience do you have that builds your credibility? This could be things like:

- Length of experience
- Key accomplishments in roles
- Client lists
- Well-known employers
- Successful projects
- Awards at work
- Partners you worked with
- History of advancement
- Quantifiable results
- Size of budget managed/worked on
- Size of team that you lead
- Specializations or focus areas
- The scope of your roles (global, international)
- Working on well-known brands or products
- Volunteer work
- Additional experience (non-profits, committees, etc.)

As you list your experience, also consider if you can creatively position any of it to bolster your personal brand. For example, I attended an innovation workshop where the leader "invented Baked Lays," another friend "Launched Well-Known Brand in Canada," a colleague "Saved Brand X from Discontinuation," and a client "Tripled Profitability of Company Y." In all of these cases, work achievements were positioned creatively to create compelling speaking points.

 Remember:
There is a big difference between creative positioning and dishonesty. Never put your credibility into question by being dishonest or misleading.

Credibility

Often times business professionals find that they also have credibility boosters beyond their experience. These could be other things that you participate in or have done that you can highlight.

Are there other credibility boosters you can highlight? This could include things like:

- Contributing to articles
- Contributing to books
- Industry recognition of your work
- Celebrity associations
- Participating in an association
- Board or committee participation
- Attending or participating in industry conferences
- Media appearances
- The scope of your work (e.g. International)

Accomplishments

Other accomplishments can also be used to establish your credibility. Consider other things that you have done/achieved that could be relevant to your personal brand positioning.

Do you have key accomplishments that you can highlight to grow your credibility and believability?

- Awards
- Speaking engagements
- Writing articles for industry publications
- Authoring books
- Earning scholarships
- Education
- Certifications
- Courses
- Extra-curricular activities
- Achieving a record at something

Depending on where you are in your career you may have accomplishments focused on your education and skills demonstrated in part-time work, extracurriculars, and internships, or you may have a variety of experiences and accomplishments to pull from. Regardless of how much experience you have, take the time to position it as competitively as possible. Over time, as you gain more experience you can add to your list.

Big Idea
You can also qualify your accomplishments to make them even bigger. Instead of "author" I am a "bestselling author." Instead of "speaker" I am an "international speaker." This can add even more credibility to how you position your accomplishments.

Think broadly about all of the things that you have done and how they could best be positioned to get people excited. If you have your résumé handy use that to jog your memory, but also think beyond things that you would typically include on it.

Action:
The key to success is strongly positioning the things that bring you credibility. Take some time to consider your experience, credibility-boosters, and accomplishments and choose the strongest ideas to include in your brand.

Based on the ideas from your MADE (Memorable, Authentic, Different, and Educated) brainstorming above, choose 5–10 key elements that you want to highlight. Based on your personal brand objectives there may be different sections that are more relevant to you.

For example, if your aim is to become a coach, building a personal connection is really important, so you may focus on the A bucket and the D bucket to differentiate yourself in a crowded marketplace. If your goal is to gain a promotion where you work, you may aim to focus on the D and E to standout more vs your peers. If you want to increase sales, you may focus on A and E to build relationships and establish your credibility as a thought leader.

Aim to choose no more than ten, and fewer than five is okay as well. Try to incorporate one element from each of the MADE categories to craft as strong of a brand as possible. You may notice some overlap in your ideas, which is okay

DETERMINE YOUR BRAND BUILDING: MADE

➢ What makes you memorable?
➢ How can you bring your authentic self across?
➢ What differentiates you from others?
➢ How can you showcase your credibility?

_____

_____

_____

_____

_____

_____

_____

What is the big thing you want to remember from this chapter?

_____

_____

Go to www.LaunchYourself.com/book for your free action planner and bonus resources.

CHAPTER 8: DEFINE YOUR BRAND CHARACTER

Brand character is where you bring your brand personality across. This is what leads to a deeper and more personal connection that drives people to relate to and like you. Many make the mistake of thinking that a professional brand is all professional, but that couldn't be further from the truth.

Different brand characters can work – even for the same objective or in the same profession. The key to a successful character is making sure that it is authentic and natural to you, and that you can be consistent in bringing it to life.

Brand character is the personality that drives your brand. Even consumer brands have this. Consider the different brand personalities between Starbucks and Dunkin Donuts.

Starbucks is serious and sophisticated about the love of coffee. The brand personality is stylish, wealthy, and they definitely take coffee seriously. Starbucks loves the finer things and doesn't compromise.

Dunkin Donuts is quirky and fun. They are relatable and about the enjoyment of coffee (and donuts!) in a fun and light-hearted way. They aren't serious, they are about value – and enjoying life.

The images below from the brands' Instagram accounts show the difference in personality and character from two brands selling basically the same thing.

Even with very different personalities, both are wildly successful brands.

Consider the personality differences between Oprah Winfrey and Ellen DeGeneres. Both have successful talk shows and share advice and opinions with their audiences. Oprah positions herself as a sage – a wise woman who is sharing her knowledge with you. Her brand positioning is kind, but more serious and professional. Ellen, on the other hand, is a jester and a comic. She is funny and quirky and uses comedy to get her message across.

With both women, a quick look at their profile images shows their different personalities or characters shining through. Both are smart and smiling, but there is a different feeling you get from the quirky Ellen style vs the sage Oprah style.

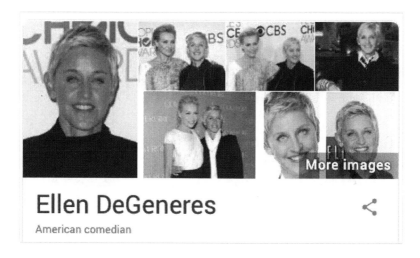

Ellen DeGeneres
American comedian

Oprah Winfrey
American executive

Don't think of this as a character that you play, rather how you want to be perceived. Consider the differences in character between Steve Jobs and Bill Gates or Martha Stewart and Rachael Ray.

As you execute or deliver your personal brand you'll want to be as consistent as possible in how you represent yourself, so defining your intended character upfront is important.

It isn't that one-character style or approach is better than another – it is about finding one that works for you and deliberately building on it.

BRAND ARCHETYPES

Brand archetypes are one of the best ways to think about the brand character that you want to create for yourself. An archetype is simply a typical example of something. As we think about brands, the 12 brand archetypes are the most typical personalities or characters of brands that you will find.

As you think about brands that you know and love, you'll probably be able to easily characterize them as one of these archetypes. Weaker brands are usually more difficult to place, as they are less clear in their positioning and distinction. As you think about brands, you'll also notice that some types are more likely to fall into different archetypes. For example, luxury, indulgent food brands are typically the lover (think Godiva, Magnum).

Big Idea
It may be difficult to choose s single brand archetype for yourself, but by choosing one you can create a stronger and clearer brand. As you review the archetypes, try to see which one you naturally fit into.

Brand Archetypes

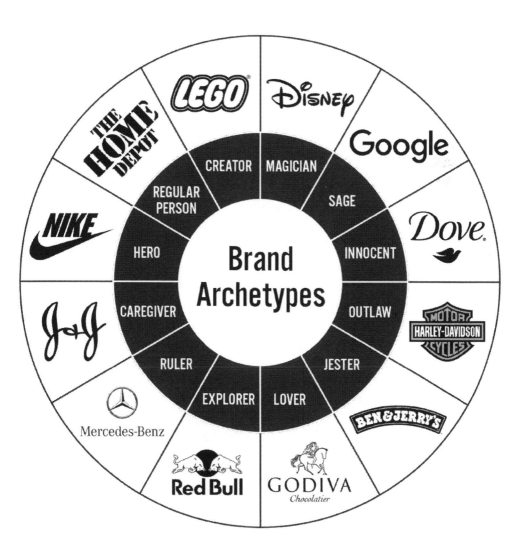

1. The MAGICIAN – I make dreams come true
Examples: Disney, Wizard of Oz, Apple

The magician doesn't create a brand to help you do something better – the magician brings your dreams to life. Disney is actually a media company, but it is in a class of its own vs. other media companies because it offers a transformative experience.

Goal: Make dreams come true, create something special, craft a memorable experience.

Traits: Enchanting, visionary, charismatic, imaginative, idealistic, spiritual, magical

Marketing Approach: Inspires change, expands consciousness, helps people transform, takes you somewhere special

2. The SAGE – I help the world gain wisdom and insight

Examples: BBC, Harvard, PBS, Google, Philips, Oprah

For the sage, wisdom is the key to success. The sage values knowledge and commands respect by demonstrating brilliance. They impart knowledge, understanding, insights and wisdom onto others.

Goal: To help people gain insights, knowledge, and understanding.

Traits: Trusted information source, knowledgeable, wise, intelligent, mentor, advisor, thoughtful, analytical, guide.

Marketing Approach: Provides trusted, knowledge-based information and products to help people better understand the world.

3. The INNOCENT – I want everyone to be happy.

Examples: Dove, Toms, Coca-Cola, Burt's Bees, Orville Redenbacher

The innocent is free, happy, content, and virtuous. The innocent doesn't make you feel guilty; instead they charm you with happiness and nostalgia. Innocent is selling you a treat, simpler and happier times, and joy.

Goal: To be happy.

Traits: Loyal, pure, young, optimistic, good, simple, moral

Marketing Approach: Provides strong values without a guilt trip, reminds you of simpler and happier times, reliable and honest, simple, associated with morality.

4. The OUTLAW – I want a revolution!!!!

Examples: Richard Branson, Virgin, Harley-Davidson, Diesel

The outlaw isn't afraid and is excited to drive change and individualism. The outlaw stands out from the crowd by going against the grain and doing something different. Be yourself and don't accept the status quo.

Goal: Break the rules and fight authority.

Traits: Against the grain, fighting for change, breaking the rules, rebellious, standing for something different

Marketing Approach: Provides a message of change for those disenfranchised. Challenges the status quo and invites people to break the rules and join the revolution.

5. The JESTER – I will make you laugh ;-)

Examples: Ben & Jerry's, Skittles, Sharpie, Taco Bell, Jim Carey, Ellen DeGeneres, Old Spice

The jester relies on humor, silliness, and nonsense to connect. The jester aims to make you smile with light-hearted fun and humor. The charm of the jester is in turning things into jokes and creating happiness.

Goal: To be happy.

Traits: Sense of humor, fun, getting into mischief, fun-loving, funny, "good time guy", spontaneous.

Marketing Approach: Helps people enjoy what they are doing and have a good time doing it. Spontaneous and impulsive.

6. The LOVER – I will make you mine.

Examples: Godiva, Magnum, Victoria's Secret, Chanel

The lover relies on passion, pleasure, and sensuality. The lover brand aims to seduce you and be a part of the intimate moments in your life with decadence and indulgence.

Goal: Create intimacy and inspire love.

Traits: Romantic, sensual, seductive, passionate, intimate, warm, idealistic, decadence.

Marketing Approach: Enjoy intimacy, make moments better, build relationships, feel appreciated, belonging, and connected. Passionate.

7. The EXPLORER – I will make you free!

Examples: Red Bull, Subaru, Jeep, Indiana Jones, North Face, Lonely Planet

The explorer prioritizes freedom over comfort and exploring over security. Other brands may help you build a home, the explorer will get you out of it. Decide where you are going and choose your destiny no matter the circumstance. Experience new things.

Goal: Discovery and experience new things.

Traits: Adventurous, pioneering, risk-taking, curious, independent, restless.

Marketing Approach: An authentic brand that helps people explore and builds a sense of excitement through freedom and adventure.

8. The RULER – I have the power.

Examples: Mercedes, Microsoft, Barclays, Rolex, IBM

The ruler is the gatekeeper – with the perception of high-quality and exclusivity, the ruler has power. Ruler brands are often high-end products like jewelry, market leading software, and high-end vehicles.

Goal: Create order from chaos. Control.

Traits: Responsible leader, organized, role model, authoritative, administrator.

Marketing Approach: Creating stability, order, and security in a chaotic world. Help people become organized and restore order.

9. The CAREGIVER – I will nurture you.

Examples: Campbell's Soup, Heinz, Johnson & Johnson, Mother Theresa

The caregiver wants to be there to help and support you. They are trusted, kind, and benevolent. They aren't confrontational – they are supportive and nurturing.

Goal: To care for and protect others.

Traits: Nurturing, generous, selfless, caring, compassionate, supportive.

Marketing Approach: Helps people to take care of themselves and focus on helping, supporting, and nurturing people. Kind and compassionate.

10. The HERO – I can (and will) do it!

Examples: Nike, Duracell, BMW, US Army, FedEx

The hero helps the world by being the best. They will help you to rise to the occasion and are there to challenge you. The hero is courageous and is there to save the day!

Goal: To help improve the world.

Traits: Confident, strong, self-assured, courageous, bold, brave, inspirational.

Marketing Approach: Makes a positive mark on the world by solving problems or inspiring others to.

11. The REGULAR PERSON – I want to belong.

Examples: Folgers, Home Depot, eBay, KFC, Ford

The regular person is an everyday person just like us. They aren't pretentious or especially gifted – they are normal and appeal to broad demographics. They aren't hip, expensive, high-quality. They are simple and accessible. Politicians often use this archetype to become relatable.

Goal: To belong or connect with others.

Traits: Guy/girl next door, accessible, down to earth, connects with others, folksy.

Marketing Approach: This marketing approach is to be accessible, and blend with average people. It gives a sense of belonging by being common and "just like you."

12. The CREATOR – I want to craft my perfect vision.

Examples: Lego, Crayola, Apple

The creator isn't worried about cost – they want to bring their vision to life. While the magician is imaginative the creator wants to create something you can't live without. The creator builds something new and inventive.

Goal: Create something meaningful that lasts.

Traits: Creative, artistic, inventive, imaginative, entrepreneur, non-conformist.

Marketing Approach: Helps customer to express or create and foster their imagination. Visionary and bringing new experiences and ways of thinking, doing things, or products.

Brand archetypes are often used in branding exercises to help brands to see themselves and choose a direction to consistently build upon. This is also helpful for personal branding. The brand archetypes also apply to people.

Consider which archetype applies to your personal brand? Which archetype appeals to you and authentically represents you?

Tool: Personal Brand Archetype
To help you evaluate yourself we've created a free online personal brand archetype evaluation. Go to **www.launchyourself.com/quiz** to find your personal brand archetype.

Personal Brand Archetypes

Action:
Determine the brand archetype that will be most prominent for you in building your personal brand.

You may be inclined to choose more than one, and you may see parts of yourself in all of the archetypes. While most of us are complex and are represented by more than one archetype, it is helpful to choose a primary one to give your personal brand a clear position.

TONE OF VOICE

Tone of voice is the tone that you take when communicating with others. This isn't about what you say but how you say it. It is like the color, font, and "look and feel" of design, except for language.

This should be linked to your personal brand archetype in a natural way. A Sage shouldn't have a ton of voice that is too humorous, for example.

The clearer and more distinctive your tone of voice, the more likely you are to create a strong brand. As you look at other strong brands, you'll typically find that they have a distinctive and consistent tone of voice.

Power Tip:
Just because you are in a serious profession doesn't mean that you have to be serious. Consider Dr. Phil who I would classify as an Average Joe archetype. He is casual, simple, and clear in his language and "tells it like it is." He makes complex topics understandable and relatable.

What tone of voice will you use? What type of language is appropriate?
Direct and to the point? Storytelling? Funny? Raw?

Action:
Determine the tone of voice for your personal brand. Look at examples to get a feel for what is and isn't appropriate for your tone of voice based on your personal brand archetype.

HOW SHOULD YOU MAKE SOMEONE FEEL?

After selecting your archetype and tone of voice, consider how someone should, ideally, feel after interacting with you.

- Inspired?
- Safe?
- Secure?
- Curious?
- Motivated?
- Smarter?
- Prepared?
- Loved?
- Seduced?
- Understood?
- Nurtured?
- Heard?
- Organized?
- Right?
- Knowledgeable?

As you create content and begin executing your brand, having a clear idea of how people should feel can help you evaluate if your brand is connecting and driving the impact that you want.

DESIGN YOUR BRAND CHARACTER

➢ What is your primary personal brand archetype?
➢ What is the right tone of voice to bring it to life and connect with your audience?
➢ How should someone feel after interacting with you?

_____

_____

_____

_____

_____

_____

What is the big thing you want to remember from this chapter?

_____

_____

Go to www.LaunchYourself.com/book for your free action planner and bonus resources.

CHAPTER 9: DESIGN YOUR MISSION

Now that your brand building blocks and character are clear, it is time to define your brand mission. Your mission, should you choose to accept it, is your driving force. This is your **"why."** So far most of our focus has been on how you do what you do. Now we want to focus on why you do it.

Your mission should get other people excited and inspired to join you! This is your emotional calling and why people will become a part of your tribe and support you.

A lot of personal brands do the work on the branding and positioning but forget the mission. While it is important to have a clear elevator pitch that explains who you are and what you do, that isn't going to get people excited to be a part of it. The mission is vital if you want to bring people with you on your journey.

FINDING YOUR WHY – THE GOLDEN CIRCLE

Simon Sinek has one of the most watched TED Talks about finding your why and what he calls the golden circle. The idea is that most businesses or people are able to easily describe what they do – this is the product or service that you provide to your audience. The next level in is how you do it. This is what differentiates you from your competitors, and we spent time on this in the personal branding statement and the brand building blocks. How do you do things in a way different from others? The most important part though, and the thing that will really inspire people to follow you is the why.

Your why is your purpose, cause or belief. This is the reason that you do what you do and it will inspire others to join you.

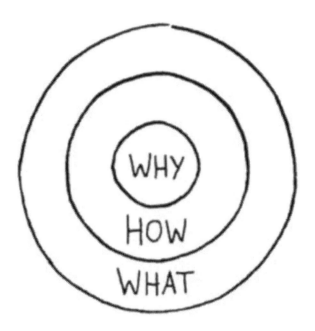

Your why is what defines your mission. Why are you doing what you do and how can you articulate it in a way that will inspire others to join and support you?

CRAFTING YOUR MISSION

Your why or your mission should not focus on you – it should focus on the people that you benefit or impact. While you may have a goal of earning income or becoming famous or accomplishing something specific, that is an outcome of your why and an outcome of your mission. My mission is to help businesses get better ROI on their digital marketing – to fulfil this I want to reach as many people as possible, which drives me to opportunities like writing, speaking, and consulting. My driving force is my mission – not the outcomes that I gain.

You'll note that all of the sample missions are written in the context of the person they benefit – not the person with the mission. It's not about YOU. It's about THEM.

Sample missions could be:

- Make stuff that improves lives (programmer)
- Help small businesses thrive (consultant)
- Give people financial stability (financial planner)
- Empower people to live their dreams (financial planner)

Some people create an even better and more powerful mission by quantifying it.

For example:

- I want to help over 1,000 Americans to own their own home.
- I'm on a mission to cultivate the self-worth and talent of young girls in America.

- I'm on a mission to inspire my students to be more than they thought they could be.

Action:
Craft your personal brand mission. Don't worry too much about the language at this point – you'll find and improve the words you use over time. For now, focus on the message and the benefit. Run it by a few people to see if it inspires them to want to be a part of it.

CRAFTING YOUR STORY

Once you know your why, it can also be helpful to craft your story. How did you get to be where you are? What motivated you on your mission?

Studies show that people remember stories more than statistics or almost anything else. As you start to bring your brand to life and share your mission, people will want to know your story. Why did you decide to go in this direction?

When I started my training company my story was simple. I had worked on multi-million-dollar budget brands, and then I switched gears to work for an internet startup. With almost no budget we were able to use social media to compete against businesses 100 times the size of ours. Social media was an equalizer – it was about outsmarting, not outspending. I wanted to help more businesses learn how to use social media to grow – even without huge budgets.

Your story should explain how you got to where you are and what inspired you along the way.

When I think about my personal branding story and why I teach personal branding (and wrote this book) it's because I was totally blown away at the opportunities that I was able to generate from my personal brand. I stumbled in to a lot of it, but I spent years evaluating the success formula so that other people could have the same success that I had. I want to help business professionals to generate freedom and opportunities by building a strong personal brand.

Think about your story. Why do you have your mission? What got you to where you are? What "triggered" you to decide that what you do is important? What inspired you? Your story should be true and authentic. Really think about what motivates you.

DESIGN YOUR MISSION

> ➤ Why do you do what you do? What is your motivator or driving force?
> ➤ How can you explain your why in a way that inspires others to join you?
> ➤ Can you tell a story that helps people understand your why?

_____

_____

_____

_____

_____

What is the big thing you want to remember from this chapter?

_____

_____

Go to www.LaunchYourself.com/book for your free action planner and bonus resources.

CHAPTER 10: DESIGN ELEMENTS

Design elements are how you package and present your brand. Depending on how and where you plan to bring your brand to life, you'll need different design elements. The design elements are the visual look and feel of your brand. This includes how you look and present yourself in person, as well as the assets that you craft for online, business cards, or other purposes.

It may not seem like it, but most established celebrities, authors, and well-known people have very carefully crafted design elements to bring their brand building blocks and character to life.

CHOOSING A LOOK AND FEEL FOR YOUR BRAND

Start by choosing a look and feel for your brand that matches your brand archetype and how you want to make people feel. There is no right or wrong look or feel – the idea is to bring to life the brand that you intend to create.

Look at some different personal brands online or explore Pinterest. You can also collect examples of brands, fonts, images, graphics, or quotes that describe the look that you are going for. The idea here is to compile visual assets that demonstrate the visual look and feel of your brand.

Jay Baer (**www.JayBaer.com**) is a professional speaker and a consultant who specializes in word-of-mouth and online marketing. A look at his personal brand shows some clear design choices and they are consistent across all of his platforms.

He uses purple and orange (I know you can't see it in the black and white image) and he even has a signature plaid pattern that he wears in his suit and features in his background. His profile photos are always smiling – almost as though you are catching him mid-laugh. He has a logo that is used everywhere and a clear tagline. While he uses many different photos of himself across platforms, the look and feel are consistent.

As a professional speaker, he has a logo, tagline, color scheme, and more, which you may or may not need for your own personal brand. What you do need is a clear and consistent look and feel to your brand, including how you choose to dress and look, to deliver a consistent visual brand.

DESIGNING YOUR PROFILE PHOTO

Prior to creating your design assets, it is usually helpful to determine the look and feel that you want for your brand. Start with your profile photo. Look at different pictures of yourself and determine which one best represents the brand that you are trying to create. If you don't have any that work for you, try one some different outfits and take some new pictures!!!

Consider the style of the photo, your outfit, your hair, accessories, makeup (if applicable). What representation of you best embodies your new personal brand?

When I evaluate my own photos, I can see a very different look and feel in them. Some are softer others bolder. Each one sets a different tone for my brand.

Don't pick apart the perfection of the photo or the details of how you look, focus on the overall style, look, and feel of the profile photo that you want to use for your personal brand.

Power Tip:
In your profile photo you should always be smiling, and the profile photo that you use should emphasize your face. For LinkedIn you want to crop so that at least 60% of the frame is your face. Natural photos work best.

Remember:
Your personal brand may evolve and change over time. Choose what works best for you now, and every few years you can refresh.

Your profile photo is the starting point for the visual design of your personal brand. It should match your personal brand archetype and set the tone for how you want your brand to look and feel

---

DESIGN ELEMENTS TO CREATE

The design elements are the key visualizations of your personal brand – the things that visually bring your brand to life. Depending on how you plan to deliver your brand you may have more or less visual design elements needed. For example, a CEO or business professional may not need a logo for their personal brand, but a speaker or consultant likely will.

The design elements to consider creating are:

- Profile photo
- Outfit/personal style
- Hair style
- Font

- Color scheme
- Logo
- Representative images
- Tag line

DESIGN YOUR PERSONAL BRAND ELEMENTS

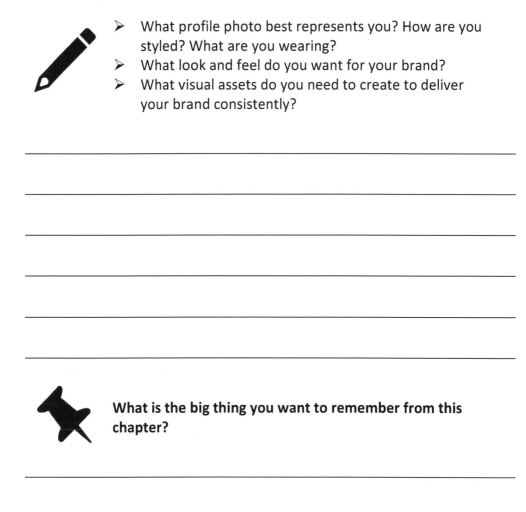

➢ What profile photo best represents you? How are you styled? What are you wearing?
➢ What look and feel do you want for your brand?
➢ What visual assets do you need to create to deliver your brand consistently?

_____

_____

_____

_____

_____

What is the big thing you want to remember from this chapter?

_____

_____

Go to www.LaunchYourself.com/book for your free action planner and bonus resources.

PART 4: DELIVER YOUR PERSONAL BRAND

Now that you've defined and designed your personal brand, the next step is gaining visibility and bringing it to life by delivering your brand.

When it comes to delivering your brand, your goal is to gain visibility with the right people to achieve your objectives. It isn't about reach or becoming "famous" – it is about crafting meaningful connections with the people needed to help you achieve your objectives.

This section will focus primarily on delivering your brand using online channels. The internet and social media allow you to develop a platform that can reach many people quickly and efficiently. This means that anyone – not just celebrities – can become an influencer or have a relevant and meaningful presence online.

Big Idea
This section will give you many ideas about how to gain visibility for your brand. Don't feel that you need to do everything Choose the most relevant and impactful areas for you based on your objectives. If your brand is a revenue source (author, speaker, coach, consultant, entrepreneur, business development) you may implement more elements.

As you start delivering your brand, keep in mind the four elements of a strong brand (MADE), as these principles should be consistently used in your delivery to maximize impact.

4 Elements of a
WOW! Brand

Memorable
Will people remember you after they meet you? Is your brand singular and simple?
SPECIFIC • SIMPLE • CONSISTENT

Authentic
Does your brand match who you really are, and come across as genuine?
REAL • STRENGTHS-BASED • PERSONALITY

Different
Is your brand specific and unique?
Do you stand out?
UNIQUE • POINT OF DIFFERENCE • SPECIALIZATION

Educated
Is your brand credible and believable based on your actual background, achievements, etc.?
EXPERIENCE • CREDIBILITY • ACCOMPLISHMENTS

The steps to building a strong brand can actually be applied to both your in-person brand and your online brand. Our focus will be online, but you can use it for both.

The steps to building a strong online brand are:

1. **Audit Yourself**
   Evaluate what you are currently doing to determine what works and doesn't work. What should you start, stop, and continue?

2. **Avoid Issues**
   Determine if there are any issues that you specifically need a plan to avoid. Consider creating your own policy.

3. **Content Plan**
   Craft your content plan or an idea of the content that you will post. What topics will you cover and how often?

4. **Build a Presence**
   Build your presence deliberately and powerfully on the networks with the biggest impact.

5. **Grow Your Audience**
   Grow your reach and impact by connecting with more people.

6. **Post, Participate, and Gain Visibility**
   Participate and connect with other people – post content, share ideas, and participate with the community.

7. **Analyze and Optimize**
   Analyze what is and isn't working and continue to build and refine your plan and execution. Your personal brand is a living thing that can (and will) grow and evolve as you do.

CHAPTER 11: BRAND BUILDING IN-PERSON

While most of this section focuses on online brand building, it's important not to ignore the impact in-person brand building can have. It often forms long-lasting connections with people.

When it comes to in-person branding the same principles apply – your brand should come across as memorable, authentic, distinctive, and credible. Building a consistent impression online and offline is important, and in-person interactions are often deeper and more memorable than online only.

In-person and online brand building work best together. For example,

- when you meet someone at a networking event you can strengthen the connection by connecting on LinkedIn or other social networks,
- if there is a prospect you are trying to close, you can follow and interact with them online to build your reputation with them,
- if you want to build a stronger relationship with your existing clients, connecting with them on social media can continue to build your credibility with them, and
- you can extend the impact of a speaking event by having the audience connect with you online.

A strong in-person brand will attract opportunities to you. By putting yourself out there in a professional and consistent way and being clear on what you want, you can create many opportunities to attract people with your personal brand.

Example:
The first time I attended an industry conference I was nervous – I didn't know a single person and went with the objective of promoting the startup I was working on. I went with three clear goals. The first was to liveblog to gain exposure for myself with attendees online. The second was to meet ten new people every day. The third was to meet the conference organizers and angle to pitch myself as a speaker next year. With a clear goal in mind I was able to achieve all three. By having a networking goal, I pushed myself to meet new people in every setting: waiting in line for registration, waiting for a session to start, during breaks and events, after sessions, etc. I also introduced myself to every speaker and complimented them after each session, strategically passing them a card. I made a point to meet the network organizers, and I actually got introduced through someone I talked to while waiting in line. They asked me to speak the next year.

Power Tip:
Be deliberate in your in-person personal branding and set clear goals for yourself. Think about the opportunities you have (big or small) and how you can use them to maximize your visibility. Challenge and push yourself to do more with every opportunity you have. You may be surprised at what you can do and the results.

IN-PERSON BRAND ELEMENTS

Your in-person brand should have the same strong and distinctive representation as your online brand. Whether you primarily network with people in an office environment, clients, through your public image (e.g. a CEO, online personality or speaker), or through networking events, bringing your in-person brand to life in a compelling and consistent way is vital. By thinking about your brand in advance you can make sure that you always put your best foot forward.

Keep in mind your brand pyramid and especially your brand building blocks to incorporate naturally into you in-person branding. For example, when I tell a story I may link it to a proof point that I want to seed; "when I wrote my latest book, I noticed…." "When I was in Brazil recently for a speaking engagement…" The key is to do this in a way that is fitting to the conversation and doesn't come across as bragging or changing the topic of the conversation. It may take practice, but finding natural ways to integrate your MADE brand building blocks into conversations can help bring your brand to life in a powerful way.

Some of the assets you need to bring your brand to life are:

- **Introduction** – How will you introduce yourself? What is an appropriate 2 – 4 sentence introduction that brings your personal brand statement to life in a way that you feel comfortable and natural delivering.

- **What do you do?** – One of the most common questions you'll get is people asking what you do. Consider how to answer this in a powerful and authentic way to both people in your industry and those outside of it.

- **Physical presentation** – Consider how you want to physically present yourself in terms of your overall style. This includes hair, outfit, accessories and makeup (possibly). What physical presentation best matches the brand you want to create?

- **Tone of voice and character** – As you do in-person brand building you want to maintain a consistent tone of voice and brand character (this is why it is important that it is authentic). Pay attention and make sure that your language, tone, and overall delivery in conversations matches the tone and character of your brand.

- **Conversation entrances and exits** – If networking is a part of your plan have a few planned ways to strike up a conversation with someone new, and also exit a conversation that isn't working for you.

- **Business cards** – Make sure that you always have business cards with you. Your cards should clearly represent your brand. Depending on your objectives for your personal brand you may have your own professional business cards in addition to those from your workplace. Make sure your business cards match the personal brand that you aim to create (review them vs. your style guides).

- **Stories** – Have a few stories ready to go that are natural and help tell the story of your personal brand. These can be personal and professional and naturally fit into conversations. For example, I may mention a recent trip I took overseas; people will probably ask about the trip and I can mention it was for a speaking engagement. This allows me to interject my credibility through a story in a natural way.

Power Tip:
You may need to practice these a few times to see what feels comfortable for you. Also start trying to use them and pay attention to how people respond.

Remember:
In-person personal branding isn't an opportunity for you to talk about yourself. It should be a mutually valuable and interesting conversation – people do business with people they know, like, and trust. Aim to build all of these with authentic conversations that aren't just about you.

IN-PERSON BRAND BUILDING OPPORTUNITIES

There are many opportunities to build your brand in-person. The types of opportunities you seek out will depend largely on your objectives.

Example:
When I started trying to deliberately build my personal brand, I went to an industry conference and made a point to ask a question at every session I attended, including breakouts and keynotes. By the end of the conference multiple people came up to me to find out who I was. I created visibility for myself and attracted opportunities to me by viewing the event as having branding potential. Think of every event as a branding touchpoint – even simple meetings with your boss or coworkers – and start to look for opportunities to get these touchpoints to work harder for you.

Some in-person brand building to consider includes:

- Industry association events
- Networking events
- Local (or national) speaking opportunities
- Team or company meetings
- Client calls
- Meetings

- Speaking engagements
- Sales calls
- Local industry events
- Social settings
- Special events (internal or external)

Power Tip:
View every opportunity that you are in front of a relevant audience as a brand building opportunity. I had a coworker who made a point to ask a smart question at every team meeting. She said she made the point to stay top of mind with the larger team, many of whom she didn't regularly work with.

IN-PERSON BRANDING TIPS

Here are some tips to bring your in-person brand to life as best as possible:

- **Be consistent** – Consistency is key – be consistent in how you appear and present yourself in professional settings.
- **Be a good listener** – Sometimes we are so eager to bring our new brand across that we forget that a conversation is a two-way dialogue. Listening is a great way to attract people to you and for you to find opportunities for connection. You'll be in a better position to make yourself interesting to someone who you listen to first.
- **Be authentic** – People will remember you if they connect with you. Be genuine and authentic and look to make a personal connection with people - not just pitch them on you, your product, or service.
- **Make more of every interaction** – Every time you interact with people - at a sales call, in a meeting, at a networking event, at a company event – think about how you can make more from the opportunity. How can you use it to grow your visibility? How can you make a bigger impact?

- **Set goals for yourself** – As you interact with people or attend events, set clear goals for yourself to push yourself beyond your comfort zone and drive a bigger impact. This will also keep you focused on your reason for attending.
- **Follow up** – Follow up with every person or potential opportunity. Whether through an email with a specific next step, a social media connection request (ideally both), or a phone call or formal next steps, view the initial in-person meeting as a foot in the door and continue to work to deepen the relationship – especially if it is with someone who is strategic to you achieving your goals.
- **View everything as an opportunity** – Remember that everything is an opportunity, so present yourself that way as much as possible.
- **Don't be too salesy** – Nobody likes to feel like someone is selling to them (or at them). Remember that the best way to bring your brand to life is through natural conversation and to identify opportunities.

Power Tip:
You never know where you may meet someone who can help you achieve your goals. When I first started by business I was waiting for a friend at a lounge and a couple started talking to me (probably feeling bad that I was alone). It turned out that they had just started a non-profit and they become one of my first clients. Over the years I did many projects for them and they introduced me to others.

APPLYING THE 7 STEPS TO IN-PERSON BRANDING

We introduced the seven steps to building a strong brand online, and the same steps (with slight adaptation) also apply to your in-person brand:

1. **Audit Yourself**
   Think about your most recent in-person experiences with others. This could be coworkers, superiors, at networking events, etc. How did you present yourself? Were you memorable? How did you make people feel?

   It may be helpful to ask some trusted friends for advice here. Many people won't give you negative or constructive feedback – they will either give positive feedback or say nothing. Ask your friends for constructive feedback so that you can maybe see some blind spots of things that you aren't noticing. Most of the best insights I've gained into my personal brand have come from other people.

2. **Know and Avoid Your Issues**
   Are there any specific issues that you are looking to change or improve regarding how you interact with people in person? For example, I often get stuck in a conversation and don't know how to exit. Or I don't make enough effort to meet new people. Know the issues that you have so that you can make a plan to address them.

3. **Have a Plan + Goals**
   Set a plan for yourself at your in-person interactions. Have a clear idea of what you want to achieve and what you need to do to achieve that objective. To the extent that you can, build a plan for your talking points to feel prepared.

4. **Build a Presence**
   Try to create as much of a presence as possible at the events that you attend in a meaningful and relevant way. Be deliberate and strategic about how you represent yourself. When you are at an event aim to be as proactive and participative as possible. Proactively start conversations, talk to new people, and join conversations. Don't wait for opportunities to find you – find them!

5. **Grow your Network**
   Plan to get yourself in front of new people and grow your network. This can be both internally if you work at a company and externally. The more people who know you and have a positive impression about you the more opportunities you will have.

   Set goals for yourself at in-person interactions for how you can grow your network. Even a 1:1 meeting could provide opportunities to meet others in the organization, or gain referrals or recommendations to similar businesses.

6. **Extend the Connection Online**
   Making a great impression in-person is great! The next step is to deepen the relationship and build on it. Swap business cards whenever possible to extend the connection online through social networks. Follow up with an email and stay top-of-mind through social media.

   Many people fail to continue relationships after they have met someone. Some businesses don't even have a strong follow-up process after paying to attend a trade show. Create a process or system to follow-up with contacts that you make in person with an aim of providing them with value and deepening your relationship.

7. **Analyze and Optimize**

   Analyze what is and isn't working and continue to build and refine your plan and execution. Make a point to do a mental recap of every event: What went well? What didn't go well? Did people remember you? Were they interested in you? Did they ask you questions? Were you dominating conversations? Did you meet your goals? Did you run in to any issues? Did you gain meaningful contacts?

   Evaluate how things went and build your plan for next time. Set a few specific goals for yourself based on your analysis of your performance.

   If you have a trusted friend, colleague, or co-worker, ask them for advice. Ask them to watch and observe you at an event (as well as how people respond to you) and give you feedback.

Your personal brand is a living thing that can and will grow and evolve as you do. Pay attention to how people respond to you and remember that feedback (especially negative feedback) is a gift.

Power Tip:

A good friend of mine, Saul Colt told me that when he meets people in person, he folds back a corner of the business card, and each corner means something different. For example: top left = try to build a strong relationship with, top right = immediate sales opportunity, bottom left = interesting but no action right now, bottom right = probably not a strategic connection. When he returns from a large event where he has met hundreds of people, he can quickly prioritize his follow-ups.

Remember:
Be as clear and specific as possible about what you do and what opportunities you are looking for. Years ago, I attended a meeting for Business Networking International (BNI) which is a networking group where members refer business to one another. At the beginning of the meeting each person had 60 seconds (timed) to introduce themselves, what they did, and tell the group what type of leads/clients/referrals they were looking for. An accountant impressed me the most. Instead of just being an accountant who could do accounting for small businesses he said "I'm Bob Smith, and I love helping businesses save money and headaches by handling their books. I'm really able to drive impact with landscaping and construction businesses right now – and have had some huge client successes. If you know any of these, please let me know because I have some solid strategies to save them money." He ended up getting the most referrals that day because instead of people thinking about if they knew small businesses needing an accountant, they were excited to give him referrals to businesses that they really believed that he could help. People were excited to give him referrals and he made it easy for them because he was so specific in his request.

DESIGN YOUR IN-PERSON BRANDING PLAN

➢ What in-person opportunities can you take advantage of? Which ones should you add?
➢ What are your goals for these events? How can you maximize your effectiveness?
➢ What is your plan to strengthen and build connections afterwards?

_____

_____

_____

_____

_____

What is the big thing you want to remember from this chapter?

_____

_____

Go to www.LaunchYourself.com/book for your free action planner and bonus resources.

CHAPTER 12: ONLINE BRANDING AUDIT AND ISSUES

The first two steps in crafting a powerful online brand are auditing and issues. While these steps don't sound like fun, they are vital to creating a powerful brand for yourself.

Auditing your personal brand allows you to see how you are currently represented so you can identify gaps, strengths, and opportunities. The audit is about understanding your current digital footprint.

Your "digital footprint" is the digital information about you that is available online. It is important that you check and monitor this regularly so you are aware of any information related to you - positive or negative.

Once your audit is complete you can assess if there are any issues that you should be prepared to handle, or proactively create a plan for. This focuses on creating your own personal social media policy to identify any guidelines or boundaries that you want to create for yourself.

After you understand the current situation and how you want to guide yourself, you'll be ready to start creating your content plan.

GOOGLE YOURSELF

Start with a simple Google search for yourself. What shows up in Google results for you? Is it good? Bad? OK? Click on all of the links that show up to see what information is behind each search result. Is it something you can edit like LinkedIn or Facebook? Or is it on a third-party site that you can't control such as a news article?

Start by understanding the first impression that you are creating in Google.

Power Tip:
If you have a common name try thinking about how someone may search for you. Try your name + city, + profession, + employer, + industry. The goal is to see what someone searching for you would find.

Compare your search results to the results of people who have invested in their personal brand. Search for me (Krista Neher), Marie Forleo, Gary Vaynerchuck, or others you admire. What sets them apart? What parts of the search results have a WOW factor that you want to build for your brand?

Tool: Google Alerts
A Google alert is free to setup and notifies you whenever your name is used online. Go to alerts.google.com to create an alert that will email you when your name is used online.

AUDIT YOUR SOCIAL NETWORKS

Audit your social networks to see what shows up as a part of your public digital footprint and your "private" digital footprint. "Private" is in quotations because we know that online, nothing is really private, however you can limit visibility with privacy settings.

First, log out of all of your accounts to view the information that is publicly viewable to people who aren't connected to you online. Many people are surprised to find that things like "Pages you've liked" are viewable to people who aren't your friends. Know what information about you is publicly viewable to non-connections or friends as this is a part of your public personal brand.

For example, on Facebook even without logging in people can see some of your account information.

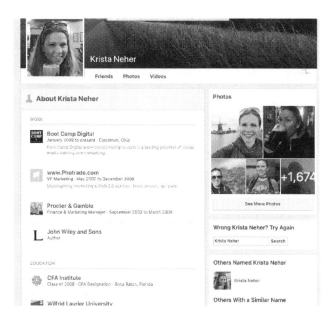

Power Tip: Check your Privacy Settings
Check your privacy settings on all social networks and make sure that you know who can see what. You can also choose to make individual posts available to different audiences on some networks – for example on Facebook a post can be available to the public, to your friends or only to lists of your friends.

Big Idea: Private vs. Personal
Keep in mind that private and personal aren't the same. You may post personal content on a private or public account, and often time accounts we perceive as private (for example Facebook) can actually be public. Assume that all content you post is or could be made public, and check that it wouldn't cause issues for you.

Next, log in to your social networks and look at the content that you post. Step back and ask yourself: if I didn't know this person, what would I think of them? Are there any specific issues with what you post? What is your content mix? Is there anything alarming? Do you post content that doesn't represent you well (e.g. negative, complaining, polarizing, etc.)?

When I first audited my Instagram account, I found that 90% of my pictures were of alcohol. Apparently, I found cocktails and craft beer to be among the more beautiful things I encountered. While I don't think alcoholic beverages

are offensive, this wasn't the personal brand that I wanted to create for myself. I was really only showing one side of my interests and personality. If I hadn't taken the time to audit my profile, I never would have noticed this.

After noticing this I created a plan for my Instagram account to create more balance in my content that was more reflective both of me and of the brand that I wanted to create. I looked for opportunities to add photos during a wider variety of events – including professional events. As a result, my Instagram following actually grew, and I was posting content that was more on-point with my personal brand.

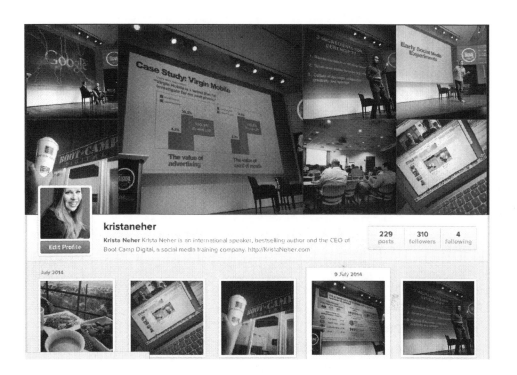

I didn't ban alcohol pictures from my Instagram account, I focused on balancing the content of my account across personal and professional topics. I brainstormed professional content that I could create and found opportunities to share.

This is where a content plan is helpful, which we'll discuss in the next chapter.

Big Idea
Often times the issue with personal social networks isn't about hiding part of your personality – it is finding authentic ways to add balance to make your online brand more reflective of who you are overall as a person.

Audit and look for balance in content on both professional and personal networks – you never know where your next opportunity might come from.

Power Tip: Personal and Professional are Blurry
Prior to the internet we used to have a lot of control over personal vs. professional relationships, as they happened in different places. With the internet it is blurry as most people have professional connections on their personal social networks. At the same time, our personal contacts are often a good source of professional opportunities. For example, many of my clients have come from friends making referrals or even becoming clients themselves. For this reason, it is helpful to view even your personal social networks as somewhat professional.

As you look at your social networks, make a "start, stop, continue" list.

- **What should you start doing?**
- **What should you stop doing?**
- **What should you continue doing?**

CREATING YOUR PERSONAL SOCIAL MEDIA POLICY

As you audited your social networks, did you find any issues? Was there content that stood out as not appropriate? If you aren't posting a lot yet, are you concerned about how certain types of posts could be interpreted?

This is where a personal social media policy comes in to play. Most businesses have social media policies that outline the do's and don'ts for their employees. The reason for this is that it is helpful to think about potential issues and develop clear guidelines to follow, vs. dealing with everything on a case-by-case basis, or worse, dealing with a reputation management situation after the fact.

The same is true with your own social media use. Creating a policy will allow you to think about possible issues or hot topics upfront and decide how you want to handle things, vs. relying on your judgement in the moment.

I created some "rules" or policies for my own social media usage to manage my professional reputation.

For example,

- I don't post content late at night because I don't want clients to think that I'm not at my best and well rested – even if I was working late.
- I don't post about drinking on weekdays.
- I don't post about politics (including comments) or religion.
- I don't post about polarizing topics.
- I almost never complain about businesses online.
- I aim to compliment nine businesses for every one complaint.
- I avoid negative content and have a 90% positive policy for my social networks.

Your social media policy is only for you, so think about what is helpful to you. Some things to think about for your personal social media policy:

- What times of days are off-limits for posting?
- How do you feel about posting pictures with alcohol? Or drugs?
- Is certain content not appropriate for weekdays?
- What language is off-limits?
- What is your guideline for political posts?
- What are your privacy settings (and what should they be) for different networks?
- What personal content do you post? What do you not post?
- Any other off-limits topics?
- Do you want to limit negativity in your content?
- Is complaining about businesses or people off-limits?
- Do you need to set any expectations with your friends? What do you allow and not allow on your social networks? Tagging you in posts? Comments?

This is just a thought-starter list based on the most common social media issues. You may have additional topics that came to light during your audit.

PERSONAL BRAND ONLINE AUDIT AND POLICY

➢ What information is publicly available on your social networks? How does it represent you?
➢ What are you posting on your private networks? How does it represent you?
➢ What should you include in your personal social media policy to maintain your brand?

_____

_____

_____

_____

_____

_____

What is the big thing you want to remember from this chapter?

_____

_____

Go to www.LaunchYourself.com/book for your free action planner and bonus resources.

CHAPTER 13: CONTENT PLAN

As you seek to grow your presence online, you'll begin to post and share content on social networks, and to be more deliberate about what you post. A content plan is your key to success here.

A content plan outlines the types of things that you'll post and their respective frequency. The content plan is where you bring your MADE brand building blocks to life. This is where you **show** people that you are the things that you want them to believe.

When I started personal branding, I wanted to build my brand as a social media marketing expert. This was in the early days of social media marketing. I could have simply tried to tell people I was an expert, but instead I showed them.

I started a blog sharing information about what I was doing in social media and the results. I shared content on Twitter that showed I was always reading and learning about the industry. I connected with other thought leaders and participated in their conversations. I left comments on relevant online articles. I did Amazon reviews of the books I read. **I showed my knowledge instead of telling people.**

This is the idea of your content plan – to post regular content that shows people that you are everything that you want them to believe you are. This is where you craft your plan to bring your personal brand to life online in a compelling way.

Your content plan is your roadmap for what you can post on social networks. Each network may have a different mix and style of content, but this is the overall idea of what you will post. You can adapt your plan for each network. For example, I post more personal on Facebook vs. LinkedIn.

Power Tip: You Have Great Content to Share
Some people worry that they don't have great content to share – or that they aren't the expert. Don't worry about this! Sure, some people know more than you do but for every person who knows more there are millions who know less and can benefit from what you are sharing. Don't worry about "not being an expert" or that others might not like it. Just get started. Don't let anything hold you back.

Your content plan should cover:

Big Idea
Sharing or creating good content consistently will be the key to your online personal branding success. As you build your content plan, consider your day-to-day life and be sure that you incorporate real-time content (for example sharing news articles you read in the morning) as well as realistic content creation opportunities (record a 1-minute LinkedIn video each week).

1. CONTENT TOPICS

The content topic plan is where you determine the general topics that you will post about. As you think about how you want to bring your personal brand to life based on your MADE personal brand building blocks you should start by identifying different types of things you can post about.

Remember:
A strong personal brand is memorable, authentic, distinctive, and credible. Your brand should be both personal and professional to connect with people in a meaningful way. Be sure to incorporate content that will let your personality shine through and allow people to feel a real connection to you.

Prior to getting active in building your brand online it is helpful to create a content plan that outlines the type of content you will post and the frequency.

A strong content plan for a personal brand should follow the 60/20/20 rule: 60% of content should be interesting to people and helpful in building your brand, 20% of your content can be promotional, and 20% of your content can be interesting but not directly related to your business objectives.

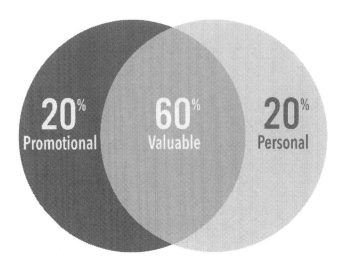

What Makes Good Content Topics?

A good content plan is about finding the content topics that grow your personal brand (meaning they build the reputation that you want to build for yourself) and they are interesting to people. For many marketers finding the balance between content that is interesting to the audience and has business value to you is a big challenge.

Some tips to craft strong and compelling content for your personal brand include:

1) **Know What's in it for the** Audience – Always ask yourself why the audience will care. What do they get that is valuable from reading this? Sometimes we focus on the things that we want to say, without thinking about how we can add value to the people we want to reach. Always add value to your audience and they will reward you with attention.

2) **Keep Your Personality Present** – Keep your personality in it. This is your personal brand, after all! Share your emotions, excitement, challenges, and disappointments. People relate to other people, so

bring your personality through in what you share and people will connect to it better.

3) **Show, Don't Tell** – When you think about what you want to communicate, look for opportunities to show what you do vs. tell them. For example, I can say "I am a social media expert" or I can show it by posting book reviews (smart people read books), sharing industry news, and writing articles. As you look at your brand building blocks (MADE) ask yourself how you can demonstrate these things in a way that is relevant to your audience, vs. trying to tell the story directly.

4) **Subtle Sales Sell More** – While you want to promote certain aspects of your personal brand, subtlety often works best. Instead of saying "I am an expert in social media," post expert social media content, share client results and discuss your thought leadership perspective. You don't have to be overt in all of your messages. For example, I may position a tip as a question that I got at a keynote presentation, to remind people that I do keynotes. If you want to hit the content sweet spot of both valuable to your audience and building your reputation, aim for subtle sales.

5) **How are YOU Represented** – A lot of people share industry news, tips, or updates from their company. These are great pieces of content, but what is missing is YOU. How are you present in these? How do YOU shine through in these updates? Think about how you can take content (for example a news article) and share it in a way that makes it your own. Maybe include your perspective, a story of why it matters, your thoughts on it, or deliver it in your unique voice. People want to hear and see you in your content.

6) **Make it Interesting** – The key to success is finding the interestingness in the content you are posting. For example, if you want to post about traveling, what's interesting about it? What stories can you share related to traveling? Maybe instead of just posting about traveling you share a business tip from the place that you have traveled to (so the travel angel is subtle). You could share a travel tip? Finding an interesting angle to communicate is the key to your success.

7) **Try Different Angles** – If you are starting out, try different angles in how you share your stories and your content. For example, I may want to share a productivity tip – I can share it in many different ways: an image with a quote, a story, just the tip, a video tip, a focus on the benefit or impact. Even when you know what you will talk about, testing different ways to bring it to life will help you discover what your audience responds to.

8) **Test, Learn, and Improve** – You won't know exactly what people will respond to right away. Be open to test, learn, and improve based on your analytics or performance. Look at what does well and why and aim to be adaptable in your approach based on the feedback and signals you get.

9) **Get Inspired by Others** – Look at others who post content that is similar to what you aspire to post. What do they do well? What makes their content interesting to you? What makes it stand out? How do they position it?

Review your Personal Brand Pyramid and remember the MADE principles as you think through the content that will work best for you. Balance professional and personal content.

Content topics are the general topics you post about, for example:

- Digital marketing news (with my perspective),
- Thought leadership ideas/articles,
- Quick tips/quotes on digital marketing,
- Personal travel/day-to-day stories, etc.

The idea is to get a rough idea of the general topics that you will post about.

You may not include all topics on all channels. I, for example, am very limited in how I share personal content on LinkedIn. But, as a starting point, think about all of the content you will post. You can customize your plan for different channels later.

Action:
Craft a list of the content topics that you can share for your personal brand. Start by brainstorming all ideas and then narrow it down to the best 4 – 8.

Content Topic Weight

Once your content topics are determined, the next step is to determine the weight of each topic. What percent of your total content should be topic make up? This helps you to make sure that you are hitting your intended balance of content topics.

Keep in mind the 20/60/20 principle – aim to create as much valuable content as possible but don't be afraid to promote yourself sometimes or post things that are not directly business related.

This may be different for each social network, or common across networks. Most people have a single content topic plan but change the % of each type of content that they post on each network. For example, my "professional" posts consist of digital marketing tips and news and make up 80% of my LinkedIn content but only 20% of my Facebook content.

Content Plan

Once you have thought through your topics and weights you can build a basic content plan. This plan should specific what you will post, the format (video, image, text) and some sample posts to remind of exactly what you intend to post.
Create your content plan. Aim to have 4 – 8 content buckets or topics that you will talk about.

Content Topic	% of Content	Format & Channel	Sample Posts / Ideas
Personal productivity tips	10%	Video LinkedIn, Facebook Page, Facebook Personal, YouTube	• 5 Things I do EVERY morning to start strong • How to minimize distractions and stay focused • The email management strategy that changed my life
Digital marketing tips	20%	Video LinkedIn, Facebook Page, YouTube	• 7 ways to make your content irresistible • Breaking industry news + my perspective • How to uncover what your customers really want (and give it to them)

Power Tip: *Be Flexible. Good Content Matters Most*
You shouldn't view a content plan as a rigid document – always focus on posting great content over sticking to a plan. The idea of a content plan is to be more deliberate about what you post – for example if I'm traveling, I may share more personal content than normal because I have some great travel photos. Likewise, at a professional trade show I may have more professional content.

2. CONTENT TYPES – HOW TO BRING THEM TO LIFE

The content type is the way that you tell the story or how you bring it to life. For example, I may have a content topic of Digital Marketing Tips. I could bring this to life in many different ways, for example:

- How to
- Case Study
- Testimonial
- Quote
- List
- Story
- Checklist
- Example

For any given topic or idea, there are many different ways to bring the content to life.

Most of us have a content type that comes naturally to us – for example I tend to focus on high impact lists or how-to's. By brainstorming different types of content, you can create more variety and may find a new one that really breaks through. Look at other people and businesses to see the different types of content that they create for topics like yours.

Action:
Looking at your content topics, brainstorm different types of content you could create for each topic. This will add variety to your content execution and allow you to explore what your audience responds to best.

3. CONTENT FORMATS

There are different formats you can use to create great content – text, images, and videos. These days, almost all digital and social media platforms include all three formats. The key to success is using each element strategically to tell your story.

Keep in mind – all of your content should consistently bring your personal brand to life and showcase your personality, tone of voice, and the elements of your personal branding pyramid.

Text

Text content is an element of almost any social media post – including videos and images. A post can be text-only or the text may accompany visuals. Text is an important communication tool as not everyone wants to watch videos and text is also readable by search engines.

Make sure that the text you use says something interesting to the audience. Don't feel compelled to use words that aren't really saying anything or adding value. For example, if you are sharing a link to an article, don't just repeat the headline, instead use the text to add your perspective or draw people in. Your text should be interesting, grab attention, and add value. Below are some tips to maximize your use of text in your content plan:

- Use as few words as possible:
    - Shorter is usually better
    - Longer thought leadership or storytelling also work
    - Keep in mind the goal of the post – don't try to say too many different things
- Add value:

- No marketing speak ("We are so excited to announce," for example)
  - What's in it for the audience?
- Organize content for quick scanning
  - Spacing
  - Bullets
  - Headers
  - Lists
- Use emojis for emphasis
- Bring your tone of voice into the text
- Have a position or point of view
- Be a real person ;-)

Images

Images are popular in most social networks – a picture is worth 1,000 words. If you are using social media to build your personal brand using real photos of real things is a powerful way to make a connection with your audience. Images are used on most social networks and accompany most other types of content – for example articles or blog posts have images, and Facebook or LinkedIn posts also perform better with images.

Power Tip: Images in Social
Images are a key part of most social media posts, and posts with images and videos perform better. Images should be a key part of your strategy to accompany text posts or articles, or the image can be the focus of the post itself.

Make sure that your images are visually telling your story – *don't overuse stock photos.*

Some tips to maximize your impact with images include:

- Visually communicate your story with ***relevant*** photos

- Make sure that you picture is contextually relevant and telling your story
- Clear focal point
  - Simple and uncluttered
  - Clear visual focus
  - High impact to draw people in
- Rule of thirds
  - Focus content into thirds to split image focus
- Less than 20% text
  - Don't overwhelm images with text
  - Text can work well for quotes or tips
- Brand elements
  - Include branding sparsely
  - Don't clutter a great image with too much branding
- Use real photos to grab attention
  - Avoid overuse of stock photos

Videos

If a picture is worth 1,000 words, a video is worth a million. Video is becoming more and more popular on more networks. It used to be that YouTube was the primary channel for video, but now people watch video on Facebook, LinkedIn, Websites, Instagram, Snapchat, and almost anywhere they can online.

 Power Tip: Video in Social
Video is powerful and performs well in almost all social networks. Most networks like Facebook and LinkedIn are emphasizing video even more, so this is a key part of any social media strategy.

The reason that video is so popular is because it allows you to build a deeper connection with your audience. Especially in the case of personal branding you want your audience to get to know you. Video allows your personality and character to shine through.

Video should be a part of your content strategy – everyone can and should record videos. If you want to see sample videos (recorded with a smart phone or computer) check out my LinkedIn (**www.linkedin.com/in/kristaneher**) or my Facebook Page (**www.Facebook.com/krista.neher.pro**).

It is helpful to have a simple plan when recording video to be sure that you stick to your point. The steps below outline your considerations when crafting a video. You don't need to create a script or a complex plan, just give some thought to each of the steps.

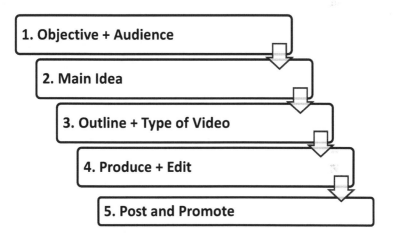

1. **Objectives and Audience:** Know the main objective of your video (what do you want it to do for you) and the audience that you want to reach. Stick to a single objective vs. trying to do too many things. For example: Showcase my thought leadership, sell my new book, share an idea, etc.
2. **Main Idea:** What is the main point of your video or the key takeaway? Social media videos generally should be short (two minutes or less) so

you want to have a clear single idea that draws people in. Determine your main idea upfront.

3. **Outline and Type of Video:** This can be as simple as outlining the three points you want to make. For example, if I make a video promoting a book, I have three things that make the book unique that I want to get across. You need a basic idea of the way your final video will look.

4. **Produce and Edit:** Create and edit your video. You'll probably be surprised that you can create a good, simple video in one take with minimal editing. That being said you can use editing software on your phone or computer to cut the video, add light animations, include subtitles, or make other improvements as needed.

5. **Post and Promote:** A video that nobody sees isn't helpful. Once the video is created have a plan for where you will post it and how you will drive attention to it. This could be through sharing on multiple social networks, tagging people, using hashtags, or even boosting or sponsoring your video to get it in front of more people.

Power Tip: Don't Script it

For the best video, don't script or rehearse (yes – I know!!!). Have an idea of your main idea and your key talking points and GO!!! You want to come across natural and authentic, and practicing and scripting will make your video seem less personal.

Crafting a great video is easier than it has ever been. Below are some tips to help you get the most out of your videos:
- Get to the point in the first few seconds
- Come across naturally
- Show your personality
- Make it interesting!
- Keep it short
  - On social networks most videos are under two minutes
  - Longer video can work but you need a great value proposition

- Have a theme
- Message is clear without audio
    - **Pro Tip:** Use captions on social networks where people have their sound off.
- Use fast cuts, moving images, and scenes
- Check your lighting (no shadows)
    - You can buy a ring light for $10 on Amazon to give you better lighting anywhere
- Pay attention to the background (less clutter)
    - **Pro Tip:** Don't record in front of a white wall or you may look like a mug shot.
- Minimize background noise
    - Use a microphone if needed

Don't let the tips overwhelm you. Go to LinkedIn and scroll through your news feed and you will find tons of people recording quick, compelling videos with no editing or production investment getting thousands (if not millions) of views.

 Big Idea: *You CAN make great videos*
Anyone can make outstanding videos for social media – you don't need a big budget or even a nice camera. Smartphones record great quality video and a selfie ring light ($10 on Amazon) can make you look even better. Include video into your strategy as soon as possible – just start recording from your computer or phone and see how much more it connects with people.

Video Types

As with other content, there are different types of videos that you can create. There are also different best practices or things that work for different types of videos.

- Thought leadership – Draw people in FAST and expand on your main value proposition. Think about breaking ideas down if needed to aim for two minutes or a maximum of five minutes.
- Unboxing – These are popular in YouTube where people show themselves opening a box with a product. These are really about personality and entertainment, and can be anywhere from 1 - 10 minutes.
- Product Reviews – I do product reviews for Amazon books that I've read. Keep these relevant and know the key points you want to make in advance. Show the product in your video.
- Live videos – Live tends to be longer since people don't always join immediately. That being said, shorter formats (10 minutes and less) tend to work best. Keep in mind that a live video can be downloaded and reused in other places also.
- Webinar – These are longer format educational videos (typically 30 – 60 minutes) and people plan to join at a specific time. These require promotion and a good topic to build interest.
- Storytelling – Tell a story with your video to share a big idea or message. Stick to important details and remember to draw people in early.
- Interview – Interview another thought leader, expert, or person of interest. Try to keep the pace moving quickly and again, shorter is better.
- How-To – These videos are different depending on what you want to teach. Some of them are 20-minute software tutorials while others are only a few minutes long. Think about the best way to show people how to achieve something, and usually a live demonstration is best.
- Tips – Short tips and tricks can be great for social media. Get to the point quickly and don't worry if it isn't very long.
- Company Culture/Personality – If you want to share something fun – that can work too! Especially on Instagram and Snapchat people love short, fun videos. If you have something interesting to share consider

creating a video that really lets your personality shine in a fun and engaging way.

- Events – If you are at events you can create short videos showing what you learned or big ideas. This is a great way to bring your audience into the event.
- Testimonials – Get testimonials for yourself (or create testimonial videos for others) to help people to see the results that they can get. Try to ask people questions and edit the video afterwards.

Want to see examples of these videos? Go to **www.youtube.com/kristaneher** and look for the video types playlist.

Big Idea: Done is better than perfect.
When I see my videos, I often think about how the lighting isn't great, I wish my makeup was better, or I flubbed a word. That is all okay. Over time your videos will improve – just get started and start sharing.

Video offers endless opportunities. Videos can also be used in many places including YouTube, Facebook, LinkedIn, your blog, your website, Instagram, and probably any other social network online. When it comes to personal branding where your personality is vital, you need video to tell your story.

Action: Create your First Video
Try it. Seriously, now. Stop reading this book and try it. Come up with a quick idea, get your phone or laptop and record a quick video.

4. CONTENT POSTING AND PROMOTION

Creating great content is the first step – getting it seen is the next. In order to maximize the reach from your content you want to have a clear plan to post and promote it.

First, know where you will post your content. Most good content can be used across social networks – for example a great video can be used on Facebook, LinkedIn and YouTube. Make sure you have a clear plan of where you will post your content.

Power Tip: Post More Than Once
Keep in mind that you can post content more than once (depending on the topic). People see a lot of content online and our memories are short. You can post a video today, and if it does well share it again in three or six months with a different description.

In order to get more ROI from the content you create, consider the following approaches to grow your visibility.

- **Post Across Social Networks** – You can post the same content on multiple networks. It is usually helpful to change the text/positioning of the content to optimize it for the network that you posted it on.
- **Use Hashtags** – On most social networks' hashtags can increase your visibility. Use relevant hashtags to make your content discoverable.
- **Tag People** – Get more exposure by tagging relevant people or pages in your content. If you were inspired by someone – tag them! If you are (positively) referencing a business – tag them! They may also share your content.

- **Promote Across Networks** – If you posted a great new video on YouTube you can also share this on other networks like Twitter, LinkedIn, and Facebook. Use social networks to promote content on other networks.
- **Re-promote** – Most content is relevant over time, and on social media very few people see every post. Change the angle of your post and talk about it again. For example, I can initial promote something with the title, then I may say "If you are a speaker or coach, you can't afford to ignore this" a week later. It is the same tip; I'm just repositioning and re-promoting it.
- **Ask for Shares** – If you have great content you can ask people to comment or share and extend your reach even further. A friend of mine just wrote a great blog post and asked me to help promote it on my social networks. He often promotes my content so I was happy to help.
- **Grow Your Audiences** – If you want your content to be seen by as many people as possible grow your audience or following on the social networks you participate in. A video takes the same amount of time to make whether 10 people or 10,000 people see it. Sharing good, consistent content will grow your audience over time.

---

5. EVALUATE AND IMPROVE

The harsh reality is that you won't know exactly what content your audience responds to until you start posting. Once you start sharing content be sure to take the time to evaluate performance and adapt your plan accordingly.

Make it a point to look at your analytics or results monthly to see what content performed best. Analyze why it performed well and adapt your upcoming plan accordingly. Recently I posted a book review that performed well on LinkedIn, so I started creating more reviews in a similar format and tagging the authors, who often re-shared.

While there are many best practices and ideas about what works to get you started, the reality is that a big part of creating great content is about finding out what works for you and your audience, and this is usually different for each person.

Take a look at your content metrics including:

- Reach – How many people who saw your content
- Impressions/Views – How many times your content was viewed
- Clicks – How many people clicked
- Engagements – Likes/reactions/comments
- Comments
- Shares
- Length of video viewed

These metrics will give you an idea of how many people are seeing your content and how they are responding to it. Most social networks now are algorithm driven, which means that if people seem interested in a piece of content then more people will see it in their news feed. So the better your content is, the more people will see it.

Don't be afraid to experiment and try new things as you get started to see what gets you the best response.

 Big Idea: Stop What Doesn't Work - NOW!
Typically, we have an idea of what we want to post or have a content plan that we start executing. Often, we post things that people just don't respond to. Few views, no comments, no shares. Yet we keep executing because it was in the plan. If something isn't working STOP IT. Find a new (more interesting) way to bring your content to life.

CONTENT PLAN

- ➤ What are your content topics and balance?
- ➤ What formats of content can you create? How can you start using more videos?
- ➤ Where will you post and promote the content?
- ➤ How will you evaluate and improve your plan?

_____

_____

_____

_____

_____

_____

What is the big thing you want to remember from this chapter?

_____

_____

Go to www.LaunchYourself.com/book for your free action planner and bonus resources.

CHAPTER 14: BUILDING YOUR PRESENCE ON SOCIAL NETWORKS OVERVIEW

Now that you know what you want to post about, it's time to start building your presence online and gaining visibility for your personal brand. Social media and a strong online presence are the best starting point.

How you use social media to grow your personal brand depends on your starting point and your objectives. For example, if you aren't active on any social networks yet you'll want to choose one to get started with. If you are already active on a few you may optimize them and then add a few more. If you are aiming to use your personal brand to earn income (coach, author, consultant, entrepreneur) you may need to build a bigger presence than someone looking to expand their reach to grow their career.

This chapter will give you an overview of the main social networks and how you can use them to grow your personal brand. If you want to learn more about exactly how each social network works in general and best practices you can check out our online training (**www.bootcampdigital.com/personal-branding-training**) or there are plenty of guides, tutorials, and blog posts available online.

The reality is that people will look you up online to establish your credibility and assess your qualifications. A great online presence does the heavy-lifting for you so that people think you are amazing before they even meet you.

THE SOCIAL MEDIA LANDSCAPE

In the early days of social media, we had a variety of complex graphics to discuss the landscape with hundreds (if not thousands) of networks. Now, social media has matured and there are a handful of big players that most people participate in.

When it comes to social networks there are six main platforms that most people consider participating in. The image below gives you a snapshot of them, their size, and the content that works for them from a business standpoint.

CHOOSING THE RIGHT SOCIAL MEDIA PLATFORM FOR YOUR BUSINESS

Facebook	Instagram	Twitter	YouTube	LinkedIn	Pinterest
2.06 billion users	**1** billion users	**20** million users	**1.5** billion users	**530** million registered users	**200** million users
Everyone	Mainstream & young users	A mix of experts and commons	Almost everyone	Professionals	Very niche, but very loyal
Images & Videos	Images & Videos	Text, Links, GIFs, Short Video	Video	Short Blogs, Infographics, Images & Videos	Images, Infographics
Solid – Best in the business	Excellent, courtesy Facebook	Decent	Robust platform High ROI	Strong – ROI not up to the mark	Good if targeted well
Clickbait & Fake News	Limited user attention span	Lack of security against trolls and abusers	Videos can be expensive to make	Largely focused on careers and jobs	Very niche demographics

WHY TO USE DIFFERENT SOCIAL CHANNELS

There are many social networks that you could use, so a helpful starting point is to understand the role each one plays in establishing and growing your personal brand.

Note: If you aren't familiar with any of these networks the Launch Yourself Planner includes Quick-Start Guides on most of them. You can find this at www.Launchyourself.com/book.

Different networks serve different purposes, as shown in the graphic below. Consider your goals and which networks are most likely to help you achieve your goals.

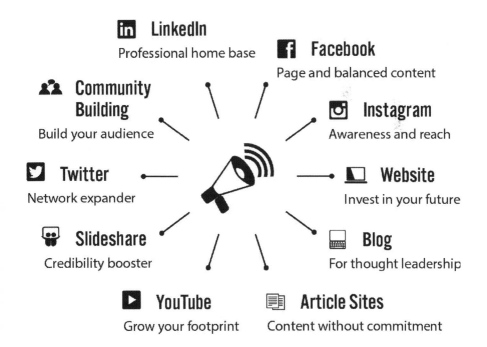

LinkedIn
Professional home base

Facebook
Page and balanced content

Community Building
Build your audience

Instagram
Awareness and reach

Twitter
Network expander

Website
Invest in your future

Slideshare
Credibility booster

Blog
For thought leadership

YouTube
Grow your footprint

Article Sites
Content without commitment

WHICH CHANNELS TO USE FOR YOUR PERSONAL BRAND

The channels that make the most sense for your personal brand will largely depend on your objectives and the amount of time that you can dedicate towards social media.

Big Idea: Do a Few Things Well
You are better off doing a few things well vs. many things poorly. Aim to launch and master one thing first, and then move on to add another.

Some people feel compelled to use all social networks to launch their personal brand, but that isn't necessary. Most celebrities with a strong presence on many networks have an entire team working for them.

When I decided to use my personal brand more strategically to gain speaking engagements, I focused on only two channels – a blog and LinkedIn. I wanted to get in front of meeting and event planners to get booked for more speaking opportunities.

Rather than trying to be everywhere, I joined meeting planner groups on LinkedIn and wrote blog posts specifically for the target audience I wanted to reach. "10 Ways to Get Your Speakers to Promote Your Event," was one of my most popular posts at that time. I wrote from my position of authority as a social media marketer and speaker and I promoted my content to groups on LinkedIn.

In three months, I generated three paid speaking engagements plus I gained additional exposure by being invited to do a webinar for the largest industry association. By having a clear goal and strategy I was able to use only two channels strategically to get tangible results.

As you think about your objectives, target audience and strategy, consider which social networks make the most sense for you based on the Cheat sheet on the next page.

What Social Channels to Use for Your
Personal Brand

in LinkedIn
Must have and must be GREAT!

f Facebook
Balance content and consider a Page

Instagram
Balance content and consider as an awareness tool

Website
If your brand is (or will be) a source of revenue

Blog
If you're serious about thought leadership

Article Sites
Try to post occasional thought leadership posts

▶ YouTube
Repurpose videos here

Slideshare
Share slideshows if you have them

Twitter
More time + effort

Community Building
Build habit to comment as you go

Power Tips

☐ *Master one channel before adding another*

☐ *Look to repurpose content across channels*

☐ *Use efficiency tools and schedulers to do more*

4 "P" APPROACH TO BUILDING YOUR SOCIAL PRESENCE

When it comes to building your social media presence there are four steps that you should plan for each social network: Profile, People, Post, and Participate. As you think about your plan, you have a setup and growth stage for a network and then a maintenance phase where you optimize and improve. Don't try to learn and grow multiple social presences at once or you may spread yourself too thin. Master one network before you move on.

Profile
• Best practices
• Bring your brand pyramid to life

People
• Grow your audience

Post
• Best practices
• Great, consistent, interesting content

Participate
• Interact
• Comment, like, share, follow

Big Idea:
As you build your social presence, be sure you plan for each of these stages to maximize your chances of success. Many people only focus on Profile and Post and don't sufficiently build an audience for their profiles.

Step 1: Profile

Build a solid profile is the first step. As you build your profile consider best practices for the platform.

A few tips for building a strong social media profile:

- Use a consistent username on every platform
- Create a square and circle version of your image for your profile picture on social networks (most require both)
- Create a background image that shows your personal brand building blocks (speaking, credibility boosters, personality shining through, etc.)
- Make sure images are the right size
- Use appealing language that will inspire someone to connect with you
- Write a clear and compelling "about" or "bio" section that explains what you do and who should follow you

Step 2: People

Once you have a profile the next step is to get people to follow you! There are many strategies and tactics that you can use to build an audience, and what works is a little different on each platform. What isn't different is that you need a clear and compelling value proposition and great content to really connect with people.

Big Idea:
At this stage it is also helpful to consider your overall strategy and value proposition for the network, as you may want to incorporate this into your profile description. Ask yourself: why should someone follow me here? What will they get out of it?

Build a plan to attract followers to your account. Beyond posting regular, compelling content, some of the most popular strategies are:

- Ads
- Email
- Community building
- Like and follow other accounts
- Contests or promotions
- In-person events
- Promote on other social networks
- Promote on your website
- Encourage others to share your content

Step 3: Post
Posting regular content that people love is important to maintain your presence and drive business impact. Each network has different norms in terms of frequency. It is important to consider how often you have great content and build your calendar around the content you have vs. an arbitrary schedule.

Tool: Scheduling
There are many tools that will allow you to schedule social media posts in advance. Most networks now allow you to create scheduled posts, but you can also use tools like Buffer or Sprout Social to schedule posts to multiple networks.

As you consider your content plan, it may be helpful to think upfront about the assets that you will need to execute. Don't be afraid to experiment with different kinds of content – especially when you are starting out.

Big Idea:
Be sure to regularly analyze your content so you know what works and doesn't. Content trends change over time and staying aware of how your content is performing as well as experimentation will future-proof your content strategy.

Step 4: Participate

Participating on social media is important – it is called *social* media for a reason. Different networks allow for different levels of interaction between business accounts and people.

For all networks you should plan to:

- Monitor and respond to comments
- Like posts or comments mentioning you
- Like other Pages when possible
- Tag other accounts
- Use hashtags as appropriate

If you really want to grow your presence you should plan to:

- Follow other accounts or add new connections
- Like and comment on posts
- Share posts from others
- Compliment and encourage other people
- Join groups or other open communities on the social network
- Give, share, and help others when you can

Most people don't build a large following just by showing up and posting content. They have a deliberate strategy to add new connections/friends.

Tool: Management

There are many social media management tools that make it easy to find and connect with others, as well as respond to comments. Hootsuite and Sprout Social are popular for this for smaller businesses, and Sprinklr is one of the more popular enterprise tools.

SOCIAL NETWORK BEST PRACTICES

Social media best practices are different for each network. Below you'll find a summary image that shows the best practices for each social network from an implementation standpoint. A few best practices to keep in mind that apply to all social networks.

- **Look, learn, and listen first** – When getting started most businesses start by posting right away. Start by listening and looking. See what content performs well. Listen to how others are interacting. Build off of the successful strategies that you can observe before creating your own content.
- **Content over calendars** – Focus on posting when you have good, relevant content for your target audience. This is more important than a schedule.
- **Content matters most** – If you don't have great content it doesn't matter what time of day you post. Focus on creating content that drives impact. Most social networks give you access to analytics, so you can see what is performing.
- **Don't be spammy** – Many social networks allow you to connect with other people and send them individual messages or tag them. Don't send private mass-messages to people – they find it annoying and you can get blocked from some networks for doing this.
- **Create on-the-go** – Get in the habit of creating great content on-the-go instead of viewing it as a task each day. For example, after you read an interesting article in the morning share it on LinkedIn and Twitter with your thoughts. As something interesting happens post a quick picture to Instagram. Building a habit of finding sharable moments throughout your day will make posting content on your social networks easier.

- **Consistent posting** – Don't expect results overnight, and make sure that you are consistent in your execution. It sometimes takes time to build an audience and get results.
- **Reply, engage, and connect** – Each network is different in terms of how businesses can interact with people, but social media should be social. Engage and interact with the people you want to reach in order to get noticed and build your following.
- **Analytics are your best friend** – Take time to review your analytics regularly so you know what is and isn't working. Many businesses don't get results because they continue to deploy a strategy that isn't generating results. Pay attention and make changes as needed.
- **Consistent presence** – Make sure that you setup a consistent presence on all social networks so that you are building a strong branded presence for your business.
- **Mobile is your best friend** – Use apps on your phone to manage your presence throughout the day when you have a few spare minutes. Post images as you take them, check in to respond to comments, get notified of comments to respond to immediately, and check in quickly to like a few updates or say something nice when you have some time.

Power Tip:
Reserve your username on EVERY social network (including those you don't plan on using immediately) so that you can build a consistent presence if you choose to add the network later.

Tool: NameVine
Go to namevine.com to see if your desired username is available. It will check the major platforms all in one search and easily allow you to consider alternatives if it is not.

Best practices in terms of content, types of posts, and frequency are usually different for each social network. The chart below shows best practices at a glance for the most popular platforms.

Following these should be your starting point, but you may find that different things work better for your specific audience.

CHOOSING THE RIGHT SOCIAL MEDIA PLATFORM FOR YOUR BUSINESS

	Facebook	Instagram	Twitter	YouTube	LinkedIn	Pinterest	Snapchat
POSTING FREQUENCY	1-4x per week	1-7x per week	2-10x per day, including retweets & replies	Weekly or when applicable	1-7x per week	3-14x per week	4-7x per week
WHEN TO POST	When relevant to audience	When audience is online	Spread throughout the day	When audience is online	During business hours	Spread throughout the day	When relevant to audience
USE OF HASHTAGS	Limited search functionality. Recommended: 1-2 per post	Recommended: 20-30 per post	Recommended: 1-2 per tweet	Use in descriptions. Recommended: a handful per upload	Recommended: 1-5 per post	Recommended: 3-5 per post	Not popularly used
BEST PERFORMING CONTENT	Photos • Videos	Photos • Short videos	Questions • Multimedia	Product Reviews • How-to Guides • Educational videos	News • Updates • Articles	Style • Home • Food & Drink • Beauty	Fun & playful • Lenses & filters
IDEAL VIDEO LENGTH	1 Minute for video 5+ Mins for Live video	30 Seconds	45 Seconds	2 Minutes	1-2 Minutes	Based on source video	10 Seconds
CONTENT TIPS	Thumb-stopping power • Short & catchy videos & images • Respond to comments	Real photos of real things • Use hashtags • Single focus of image	Mix content • Retweet • Reply and participate	Clear purpose for video • Compelling storyline • Add variety to video topics	Positive & relevant content • Add images & video • Value for audience	Variety of content • Create multiple boards • Curate content from other sources	Capture attention • Showcase business or product • Fun & light
AUDIENCE BUILDING TIPS	Post Consistent and engaging content • Boost posts	Use hashtags • Engage with audience	Tweet more often • Use hashtags and participate	Optimize for search • Post consistently	Add contacts to your network • Engage via comments and groups	Post often • Create searchable descriptions	User-generated content • Cross-promote on other platforms

Want to see the full-size image online? Go to www.LaunchYourself.com/book for your free action planner and bonus resources.

CHAPTER 15: DIVING INTO SOCIAL NETWORKS

Now that you've had the chance to see the big picture on social networks, we'll dive in to explore the social networks that are most relevant to your personal brand online. This chapter will give you an understanding of how different social networks can contribute to your personal brand along with tips and best practices.

LINKEDIN

LinkedIn is the biggest and most important professional social network. You can't afford to ignore it. LinkedIn typically shows up at the top of search engine results and it is the #1 place that business professionals go to research or learn about other people.

LinkedIn is still **the business network.** Nothing else comes close, and since the acquisition by Microsoft they've gotten more serious about rolling out new innovative features for users and businesses. With a renewed focus on the news feed, content, videos, and groups, LinkedIn is positioning itself as an even bigger and more relevant business platform.

The bottom line is that you need a great LinkedIn profile - not just a "good" or "fair" one. Everyone should have a great LinkedIn profile – even executives who have already built a strong reputation for themselves.

LinkedIn is where you build and establish your personal brand and credibility upfront.

Benefits of LinkedIn

As the biggest professional social network LinkedIn is valuable for all business professionals and also has relevant applications for sales, recruiting and job seeking. LinkedIn really isn't a job-search network anymore – it is a credibility establishing presence that can grow your reach, network and presence online and introduce you to new opportunities.

 Some of the benefits of LinkedIn include:

- **Your online résumé** – LinkedIn is basically your online résumé, but it isn't just used for job hunting. People want to understand your background before meeting you, or validate your credentials during or after a meeting. LinkedIn sets the stage for your personal brand online.
- **Always up-to-date rolodex** – People change roles and their contact information changes as they move. LinkedIn allows you to always get in touch with the people who matter to you.
- **Strengthen weak ties** – Our Facebook friends are typically the people we know best, but often our LinkedIn network includes "weak ties" or people we don't know that well. My network includes people from college, colleagues from 20 years ago, former work contacts, and personal contacts that I have lost touch with. LinkedIn allows me to stay up-to-date with these weak ties who are still relevant business connections. I stay top-of-mind with them and strengthen my relationships.
- **Stronger relationships** – LinkedIn also helps strengthen the relationships that matter. I am able to connect with, participate, and post on status updates from people in my network, which, in turn strengthens my relationships.

- **Greater visibility** – LinkedIn allows you to reach new people, as well. Content on LinkedIn can travel beyond connections to people who are connected to your network. These are called second and third degree connections. Groups on LinkedIn also allow you to reach new people and gain even more visibility.
- **New connections** – LinkedIn also allows you to reach new connections by LinkedIn search, through groups and the "people you may know" suggestions. If you want to connect with new people (sale prospects, potential customers, strategic connections) LinkedIn is a great place to do it.

LinkedIn Personal Brand Success Formula

While there are some aspects of LinkedIn that are essential to your online presence (a great profile and sharing solid content) we are starting to see the emergence of LinkedIn influencers, or people who are establishing large followings on LinkedIn by regularly sharing interesting, relevant, and useful content. Depending on your objectives for LinkedIn you can make your presence as big or small as you desire.

If you are serious about building your presence on LinkedIn you may want to post more often (daily) and focus on more video content that drives more reach.

For most personal brands, the key elements for success on LinkedIn include:

Profile
- Make it excellent (not just okay)
- Add as much relevant experience as possible
- Your profile photo matters most – make sure it is smiling and your face takes up 60% of the image
- Be sure your headline incorporates your brand building blocks vs. just state your role

- Add as much keyword rich content as possible to show up in searches
- Keep settings as open and public as possible
- Use paragraph + bullet format for text sections to drive impact
- Include "other" sections to highlight credibility (certifications, projects, etc.)

People
- Add as many **relevant** connections as possible so that your updates reach more people
- Look at "people you may know" on a regular basis
- Add people through email and your contacts list
- Add strategic business connections with a personal note explaining why you want to connect
- Request introductions to people you don't know that could be relevant for you
- Build a process to keep growing over time

Posting
- Focus on business and professional content
- 2 – 5 times a week
- Videos work great!!!!
- Tag people and pages to grow exposure
- Don't forget groups

Participating
- Comment on, like, and share others' status updates
- Interact with people who matter to you
- Compliment others, endorse skills, leave recommendations
- Send relevant messages to people (avoid spammy promotional messages that aren't customized for the person or come across as salesy)
  Join and participate in groups

How to Manage LinkedIn

The best way to manage LinkedIn is to set aside time for LinkedIn each week, and also use your phone when you have a few spare minutes.

Plan to manage LinkedIn for 15 minutes, three times a week to get started. During this time share a status update (again – VIDEO is best), add connections, review your news feed, scroll, and comment on others.

Also make sure that you have the LinkedIn app on your phone so that you can participate on-the-go and build even deeper connections with people.

FACEBOOK

Facebook is the biggest social network and more people spend more time on Facebook than any other social network. This means that if you want to regularly get in front of people Facebook is the place to do it.

Facebook is a challenge for many individuals as they aren't sure if they should use their personal profile, a page, a group, or some combination of the above. There isn't a single or simple answer to this question – it largely depends on how you are currently using Facebook and how you want to use it for your personal brand - including how much time you realistically can dedicate to it.

Since Facebook is a personal social network and most people view their personal brand as professional, many people think that Facebook isn't relevant. This couldn't be further from the truth.

Professional and personal contacts are often the same, as most people find job opportunities and clients through their friends. Also, more and more people view their professional contacts also as friends, so it isn't as simple as personal vs. professional. People on Facebook are also open to professional content – even LinkedIn advertises on Facebook for their ad platform.

I get lots of professional support from both my personal and professional connections on Facebook. Even your friends will enjoy hearing and learning about your professional successes and be inspired by the content you share. Plus, they may at some point be in a position to connect you with an opportunity.

Regardless of how seriously you want to use Facebook as a part of your personal branding strategy, you should assume that the people you are connected to on Facebook are linked to your professional success, so you'll want to at least partially use it to bring your personal brand to life.

Benefits of Facebook

More and more business professionals are using Facebook as an extension of their personal brand. Some people use it as their primary platform to grow their business and find new customers. There are a few benefits to using Facebook as a part of your personal branding strategy including:

- **Your audience is there** – Almost everyone is on Facebook, so your audience is most likely there, and they spend a lot of time there. This makes it an ideal place to grow your reputation.
- **Your friends can help** – Most people get jobs, clients and opportunities through friends. While your Facebook friends may be more "personal" in your mind, they can connect you to opportunities, but you need to position yourself well.
- **Greater visibility** – If you use a Facebook Page and advertise you can reach many new people on Facebook in a cost effective and easy way.
- **Expand your reach and network** – Many people use Facebook groups (either creating them or participating in them) to reach new people and grow their footprint on Facebook beyond their actual friends.

- **Build your reputation** – Posting regular content on Facebook is a good way to build your reputation. The challenge is making sure that it is appropriate for Facebook and not overly business or promotional. Make sure that your Facebook content comes across as personal and authentic vs. too business focused.

Your Facebook Presence: Profile, Page, Group

When it comes to your Facebook presence you'll need to determine if and how you will use your profile, groups, or a Page to grow your personal brand. Each of these may have a role but it largely depends on how serious you are about growing on Facebook.

Profile

Most people already have a Facebook profile that they use personally, professionally, or both. As you consider how your Facebook profile plays a role in your personal brand, evaluate the following:

1. How do you use Facebook today? Is it all personal? Professional? Both?
2. What are your privacy settings? What can people who aren't friends with you see? Does this represent you well?
3. How are you comfortable using your Facebook profile? Are you open to connecting with professional contacts on Facebook?
4. Based on your intended use of your profile, what do you need to stop, start, and continue?
5. How often do you want to post professional content? What is the right content mix for Facebook?

Power Tip:
Do not create a second or fake account on Facebook for your personal brand. Not only is this against Facebook's terms of service, but it is also not an authentic way to connect with

people who are sharing their personal profile with you and assume that you are doing the same.

Pages

A Page is the professional presence of a business or public figure on Facebook. If you aim to create a more public profile for yourself (running for office, speaking, author, coach, entrepreneur, executive) people may want to connect with you on Facebook but not actually be your friend. This is where a Page is helpful – it allows you to have a more official public presence.

There is some debate about the role that a Page can play in your personal brand building. I've seen some people advocate that everyone should have a Page for their personal brand to elevate themselves and increase their reach. The reality is that if you don't have time to manage a Page properly (build a following, post content and reply to comments) it could actually work against you and weaken your reputation.

There are pros and cons to using a Facebook Page as a part of your strategy. The primary things to consider are:

- **Page content gets less visibility** – The Facebook news feed works on an algorithm that decides what content people will see. Facebook Pages are seen by fewer people vs. profile content – so if you post something from both a Page and a profile, the Page post will get fewer views (usually 1% of your audience or less) unless you run an ad.
- **You have to grow your fans** – If you want to establish a Facebook Page for yourself you need to grow your fans and encourage people to like your Page. This can take time and money to build.
- **Facebook presence for non-friends** – If you are building a large professional presence for yourself there will be people who want to connect with you who aren't friends and don't want to "friend request" you, but do want to follow you. Your Page is a great place for these connections.

- **Profile connections are limited** – Profiles are limited in the number of connections you can have, so popular personalities use Pages to connect with more people.
- **Uncomfortable using profile** – Some people just aren't comfortable using their personal profile, so a Page allows them to have a presence without hijacking their personal profile.
- **You can run ads** – A main advantage of a Page is that you can run ads. Facebook ads can be very targeted and inexpensive, so if you really want to reach many people or have a product or service to sell, a Page will allow you to reach more people.

Power Tip:
Before creating a Page ask yourself if you can commit to posting regularly and invest to grow the audience of your Page.

Groups

Facebook groups can be a good way to grow visibility. The main purpose of groups is for people to connect with each other based on shared interests.

For example, I participate in digital marketing groups on Facebook as well as location-based groups that I find valuable and interesting. Many people on Facebook participate in professional groups.

When it comes to groups on Facebook, you have the opportunity to create a group or participate in existing groups. Here are a few things to consider:

- **Groups have more visibility than Pages** – Posts from groups have more visibility on Facebook than Pages, so many people prefer to use a group vs. a Page.
- **Add your Friends** – Groups allow you to add your friends (yes, without their permission) which most people find annoying, but it does create an opportunity to reach people on Facebook without having to use your profile.

- **Focus on discussion and participation** – The set-up of a group is based on members and participants sharing and discussing – not just the group owner pushing content. Depending on your intentions this could be a pro or a con.
- **Wider reach** – Groups are intended to be a place for people to share interests and connect with others. People who create interest-based groups (for example "Digital Marketing Agency Owners") are able to attract their target audience into the group and reach more people.

Power Tip:
Groups can require a lot of moderation as they grow. Evaluate if you can moderate a group and encourage conversations and discussions.

The graph below summarizes the differences between a Page and a Profile.

Personal	Business Page
Profile	Page (includes Public Figure)
Friends	Fans
No advertising options	Advertising options (boosting, promoted posts)
No Insights (analytics)	Insights (analytics)
Privacy Settings	Public
5000 friends limit	Unlimited fans
Can send, receive and respond to private messages	Can only receive and respond to private messages
Better organic visibility for posts	<2% organic visibility for posts
Follow without friending	"Like" Page to see posts in news feed

How to Manage Facebook

Decide how you want to use Facebook as a part of your personal branding strategy. There isn't one thing that works for everyone. It largely depends on your goals and objectives, as well as how you already use Facebook.

Take a look at your Facebook news feed and you will likely find a range of people using Facebook for different purposes, both personally and professionally. I have some friends that post mostly professional content, and others who post exclusively personal content.

A number of years ago I gave a keynote presentation to small business owners who used Facebook (including their profiles) to promote their businesses. They were given a challenge to post and ask their friends for help. Some people immediately exceeded their targets as their friends were thrilled to help. Others got no response. Give to others and don't forget to be a real part of the network if you want others to give to you. Strong personal relationships always matter – don't let your desire to promote yourself overtake that.

Determine how you want to use Facebook and the content mix and tone that is right for you.

Big Idea
Keep in mind that on a personal social network like Facebook the strength of your actual relationships with people will also be a factor in how they respond to your professional content. Most people don't use Facebook exclusively as a professional channel (unless they have a Page) as it can be a turn-off to many of their friends.

INSTAGRAM

Instagram is the second biggest social network and is owned by Facebook. It is primarily used for sharing images and videos, and has very high engagement rates.

Businesses and personalities, in general, haven't been quick to adopt Instagram, partly because Instagram engagements take place mostly on the app – meaning people can't click on links to buy your products or read your articles unless you use an ad.

Instagram is a powerful tool for personal brand building because so many people spend so much time on the platform. The biggest challenge is that Instagram is images-only and primarily managed through a mobile application, so some people struggle to create content for it.

Instagram is especially powerful if your goal is building awareness or reach for your reputation. People on Instagram love to discover new accounts or images by exploring hashtags, so there are lots of opportunities to build your reputation easily.

One of the other things that makes Instagram attractive for personal branding is that many people have public profiles, so you can proactively find people to follow, like, and comment on as a way to build your visibility on the platform.

You may already be using Instagram personally, in which case you should consider if you want to create a second professional account (which you can do on Instagram) or use your personal account for both your personal connections and your professional brand.

Instagram Personal Brand Success Formula

Instagram is primarily an image platform, however you can also post videos, though they must be short and videos tend to get fewer views on Instagram vs. photos. To grow your personal brand on Instagram you'll want to have a visual strategy where you share images that your audience is interested in. These could be pictures that you take on-the-go at the office or at professional events, for example, or images you create for Instagram such as pictures with quotes.

For most personal brands, the key elements for success on Instagram include:

Profile
- Add all profile information
- Be sure to include a link to your website or LinkedIn in your profile if you use it for professional purposes
- Incorporate your brand building blocks into your profile description to bring your brand and purpose to life
- Use keywords in your profile that people might be searching for when looking to discover new profiles to follow
- Make your Instagram profile a "business" account which will give you access to analytics and allows you to run ads. There are no negative consequences to having a business Instagram account.

People
- Connecting Instagram to Facebook will allow you to start by following Facebook friends
- Follow people with shared interests – many will follow you back if you are posting good content
- Use hashtags in your posts to be discovered by new people and grow your following over time as people seek out others

with similar interests

Posting
- Aim to post at least once a week and up to a few times a day
- Images should be interesting and have a single clear focus
- Stories and IGTV are additional opportunities to share interesting and relevant content
- Stunning and beautiful imagery does well on Instagram, but images with quotes or text can also work
- Tag accounts and locations to make your posts discoverable
- Use hashtags to get more visibility as many people search Instagram for hashtags

Participating
- Follow other accounts and many will reciprocate
- Discover new accounts with Instagram search or by following people who follow other accounts similar to yours
- Like and comment on other photos to build your exposure Find hashtags to follow and use that are relevant to your target audience

How to Manage Instagram

Instagram is usually managed from a mobile device, but you can also schedule Instagram posts from a social media management tool like Hootsuite or Buffer.

Depending on your image strategy you may need to start looking for content opportunities or "Instagrammable moments." The key is to find relevant opportunities to share interesting moments or stories on Instagram. Many of the most popular Instagram accounts are regularly taking and sharing photos throughout their day in a natural way.

WEBSITE

A professional website is a great investment in yourself and your professional reputation. While LinkedIn is a great home base for your professional content, you don't have a lot of control over how your content is displayed on LinkedIn. If you really want to build a strong online profile for yourself a website is a must – especially if your personal brand is an income source for you.

My website is a key part of my professional brand – and it was long before I used it to generate income as a speaker or trainer. When I started building my personal brand, I used my website as a place to really bring my brand to life and highlight my accomplishments.

I promoted my site on my social networks and found that I was able to create a strong brand impression for myself online by directing people to my website. Even though my site was really just me talking about myself it was viewed as credible and was a key asset in positioning myself as an expert.

Power Tip:
If you purchase a domain to use for your personal brand you can also set up email at that address. So instead of using a Gmail email address you can use an email address from your own domain name, which makes you look more professional.

The Benefits of a Website

The benefits of creating your own website are:

- You completely own the channel so you can decide exactly how your site looks, feels, and represents you.

- You have full control over every aspect, and you can add new pages or change content as needed over time.
- If you are generating income from your personal brand you can share your product offerings, packages, or how people can work with you on your website.
- It is an investment in a long-term asset that you can use in different ways over time to promote yourself, your skills, and your business.
- Websites can be found in search engines and discovered by the people you want to attract.

Creating a Website

The good news is that creating a website is easier than ever. You no longer need to spend thousands of dollars or deal with programmers. Depending on your knowledge level you can create your own website with drag and drop tools, you can build something more customized with WordPress or Squarespace, or you can hire a professional for under $1 for a basic website. Given the cost and ease of creating a website, it is usually a good investment for most professionals who want to generate opportunities for themselves.

BLOGGING

A blog is the opportunity to create a space where you share thought leadership or longer-form ideas or content with people. A blog can be a stand-alone website or a part of a website. For most personal brands a blog is a part of their main website. My blog is at **www.KristaNeher.com/blog** and is where I share new ideas, content, and perspectives in longer format than I can on other social networks.

From a personal brand standpoint, blogs are usually used to share thought leadership content and position the writer as an expert in an area. Social networks are great for sharing short posts, but blogs are more appropriate for longer format content. The other difference is that most social networks are timeline driven – so your post is only relevant for a short time after it is posted and then it is pushed down the news feed. Blog posts exist as long as you leave them there, so they can generate traffic and readers long after they were initially written.

Many of my professional opportunities came from my blog. I co-authored a textbook because the main author wanted a co-author and had found some blog posts I had written on strategy and thought I would be a good fit. My blog is also used to drive people from social media to my website where (hopefully) they are inspired to learn more about me or sign up for my emails.

The advantage of having a blog on your site is that you control the blog and the visibility of your posts, it is a part of your website, and it can be found by search engines. This is a great way to grow your visibility.

The downside of a blog is that you have to find the time to regularly create content, and then promote the content that you create. Many people struggle to find the time or generate ideas to post regularly (ideally weekly but a minimum of monthly). Even if you create great content, you need to draw people in to read your content via social media, email, or other platforms, which requires additional effort.

Blogging can be a powerful tool, but it does require significant time and effort. Consider if blogging is something you can invest in. If you aren't sure, you may want to try starting with article sites (the next section) and grow to add a blog once you know you have great content.

ARTICLE SITES

If you have thought leadership content to share but don't want to create a blog yourself or aren't ready to make the investment, article sites are a great place to start. Article sites are websites online that allow you to create an account and contribute an article. For example, on LinkedIn you can write an article that is hosted on LinkedIn and publicly available. On sites like Medium you can also create an account and write articles.

The advantage of article sites is that you don't have to create a regular stream of content, or invest in creating your own platform. You can contribute when you have an idea. Another advantage is that these sites usually have some built-in audience, so your articles can generate some initial views without much effort on your end. LinkedIn will show your article via the news feed to some of your contacts, even if you don't make the extra effort to promote your content.

The downside of article sites is that you don't have a lot of control over your content. It's on a site that you don't own and they won't work well if your goal is to use it for lead generation or to drive people to your own site. For example, with a blog on my own site people can then explore my site, learn about me and my products, and sign up for my newsletter or a free resource. If I publish the article on Medium or LinkedIn I lose the opportunity to promote my business to my article readers.

Article sites are becoming more and more popular as many people struggle to maintain and create their own blogs. If you are newer to blogging and want to experiment, article sites are a great starting point. Once you feel that you can create content regularly you can switch you create and promote your own blog.

YOUTUBE

YouTube is the biggest video sharing site and actually also the second-biggest search engine. People go to YouTube for education, entertainment, and to be inspired. As video has become more popular on social networks and the myth of the "viral YouTube video" has been debunked, YouTube isn't as popular with many businesses and marketers, but it is still an extremely powerful channel to grow audience.

YouTube is powerful as a personal branding channel because video is a powerful way to bring your personal brand to life, and YouTube is where people go to view videos. Unlike other social networks where videos are displayed in the news feed for a few days and then become less relevant, on YouTube your videos are always findable and viewable. YouTube videos can continue to gain views for years after they have been posted.

Creating a YouTube channel (which is the YouTube name for an account) is easy and free. Once you have a channel you can start uploading videos.

Building Your Presence on YouTube

Creating a strong presence on YouTube is relatively easy – and if people are interested in your content you can generate thousands or millions of views. Generating views on YouTube isn't as simple as creating a great video and posting it. You'll want to follow the 4P approach to YouTube to maximize the exposure of your videos.

Profile
- Add all profile information
- Include a "trailer" video that will automatically play when people visit your channel

- Organize your content into Playlists so people can easily find your videos.
- Add videos posted by other accounts into your playlists as well – for example a news channel did a segment on me that I added to my media playlist.

People
- People can subscribe to your channel to be notified of your updates.
- Great content + community will build subscribers over time
- Promote your YouTube videos on other channels (Facebook, Twitter, LinkedIn, Blog, etc.) to maximize your views.

Posting
- Write a headline that people search for and that is appealing and interesting. Many people search YouTube and the title of your video is key to gaining traction.
- Descriptions on YouTube are the only way that YouTube knows what your video is about. Write longer descriptions to maximize your visibility in searches and recommended videos.
- Most videos are 2 – 5 minutes long, but they can be longer if they add value to the audience.
- Include tags and categories to maximize exposure.
- Experiment with different videos to see what works.
- Cross-post videos that you use on Facebook and LinkedIn to YouTube to maximize your reach.

Participating
- Follow other accounts and many will reciprocate
- Get notifications of comments and respond or moderate, as necessary
- Promote your account and videos on other social networks or online channels (email, website, etc.)

Remember:
Not every video you post will be a hit – test and learn to see which videos perform well. Also keep in mind that you don't need millions of views for your video to have results – you need the right people viewing them.

If you plan to use YouTube as a primary channel to build a following, you'll want to have a clear and consistent posting plan and also spend time subscribing to and commenting on other videos and accounts. If you aren't ready to fully invest in YouTube start by using it as a place to post all of your other videos and build your video presence.

SLIDESHARE

SlideShare is a website that is now owned by LinkedIn where people can share PowerPoint presentations and PDF documents. SlideShare presentations can be found in search engines, featured on your LinkedIn profile, and are also commonly found by people looking specifically for presentations or experts on SlideShare.

SlideShare is a popular site for personal branding because sharing presentations is a way to demonstrate thought leadership and expertise. Many business professionals already have PowerPoint presentations that they've created and delivered, so SlideShare is a great way to get more visibility from content that you probably already have.

Consider if you have any presentations that you can upload onto SlideShare as a way to expand your online footprint.

Remember:
The more powerful positive content you publish online the better your overall reputation is. SlideShare is an easy way to create a professional presence that will show up in search engine results.

TWITTER

Twitter is a social network where people can share short status updates about the things that are meaningful and interesting to them. What makes Twitter different from other social networks is that Twitter content is generally public and searchable – so people use it to create a public presence and interact with other people publicly. Facebook and LinkedIn are primarily close, personal networks, where we only see content from our friends or Pages we follow. On Twitter you can search for people with whom you have shared interests and initiate a dialogue with them.

Different people use Twitter differently. Many politicians use it as a way to quickly share their thoughts and opinions with the public. Business professionals use it to position themselves as thought leaders and connect with other experts. Some people use it as a news site. Others use it personally to connect with their friends or follow celebrities. Some use it to form community around shared interests.

On Twitter most accounts are open and public, which means that anyone can see your content or start a conversation with you by mentioning you. You can do the same – you can view other accounts and initiate conversations. What makes Twitter valuable for businesses and personal branders is that you can find people in your target audience and proactively reach out to them. Likewise, others who are interested in what you are talking about can find you and follow you.

For this reason, Twitter is a network expansion tool – you can find and reach new audiences. On Facebook and LinkedIn people have to find you and connect with you before you can interact. On Twitter you can proactively find people.

Twitter is also useful at events or for participating in broader conversations. For example, at an event like South by Southwest I can follow #SXSW to see what people are saying about the event, find networking events, and connect with other people at the conference. During the Super Bowl I follow #Adbowl to view responses to the ads.

The major downside of Twitter is that it generally takes a lot of time and effort relative to other social networks. This doesn't mean it isn't "worth it" – in fact many people have grown huge audiences that drive real business results from Twitter. It does mean that you want to be sure that you have the time to invest in Twitter and are confident that your audience is there before you invest in the platform.

Building Your Presence on Twitter

Creating a strong presence on Twitter is relatively easy – people and businesses can create accounts and start posting and exploring. To build your presence consider the following steps:

Profile
- Add all profile information
- Keep your description light and interesting – most people post about multiple topics on Twitter (not just business) so you can include more personality here.
- Use keywords in your description so people can find you.

People
- Promote your account on other social networks to encourage people to follow you.
- Start conversations and follow others to grow your following, slowly and naturally over time.
- Participate in industry discussions and use relevant hashtags to be found.

Posting
- Aim to tweet at least once a day and up to many times a day
- Include retweets where you repost the content of others
- Start conversations or reply to other people
- Include images and videos
- Use hashtags that are relevant

Participating
- Follow other accounts
- Reply to others to start a conversation

- Tag other users in your conversations to draw their attention

Remember:
Twitter is conversational – the more you interact with others and initiate conversations the more your account will grow over time.

COMMUNITY BUILDING

Community building is a broad term that generally refers to starting conversations and establishing relationships with people online. In terms of personal branding the idea is to build your presence or reputation with other people via a presence, comments, and dialogue on other online sites. This can be a great way to grow your visibility and reach beyond your immediate network.

When I started wanting to build my exposure and reach online, I aimed to participate in industry discussion forums. I chose two forums and made a point to answer questions a few times a week. Over time I became seen as the "expert" in the group, and people started approaching me for consulting support. I never tried to sell my services, I simply showed my expertise.

Power Tip:
Don't be spammy and overly promotional on community sites. Aim to add value and participate in the conversation that is happening. As people see the value you bring to conversations, they will be interested in you and find you online.

Community can be built anywhere, but some things that are especially helpful for personal branding are:

- Leave thoughtful comments on industry news articles

- Write book reviews on Amazon (BONUS: upload a video with your review to get even more exposure)
- Participate in discussion forums where your audience is
- Join groups and participate
- Answer questions on Q&A sites

Think about your audience and where they spend their time online. How can you become a part of the conversation they are having? How can you build your reputation with them?

PODCASTS

Podcasts have been around for many years, and still haven't gained a lot of traction or mass adoption. A podcast is similar to a radio show – except you don't need to have a station produce it. Podcasts are typically audio and are created regularly (usually weekly or monthly) around a set topic, similar to a television show. Essentially you record an audio file and upload it to podcast distribution services like iTunes or Spotify and people can listen to individual episodes or subscribe to your podcast.

Only 26% of Americans listen to podcasts monthly. While this percentage isn't huge, it is 1 in 4 people, and if your target audience listens to them, they can be a great way to build your personal brand. Podcasts are continuing to grow and gain audience. The advantage of them is that you build a loyal audience that listens to you week after week.

Many people with large personal brands have podcassts and they often use them to interview people or share insights around set topics. Tony Robins has a podcast that he uses to build his brand and reputation. I listen to a podcast called "The Life Coach School Podcast" by Brooke Castillo. She shares general life and productivity tips and also uses it to promote her coaching programs. While she doesn't overtly sell often, by hearing her great advice and results the audience becomes interested in what she is selling.

Podcasts can be a great way to build a stronger and deeper relationship with your audience since they are often 20 – 60 minutes long. They also allow you to reach new people since many people are actively looking for interesting podcasts for their drive home, workouts, or as an alternative to reading.

The downside of podcasting is that it can be time consuming to create regular podcasts, load them online, and build an audience. Many people have had podcasts provide them with a big platform that has helped to launch their personal brand, but it took time and investment.

SOCIAL NETWORKS

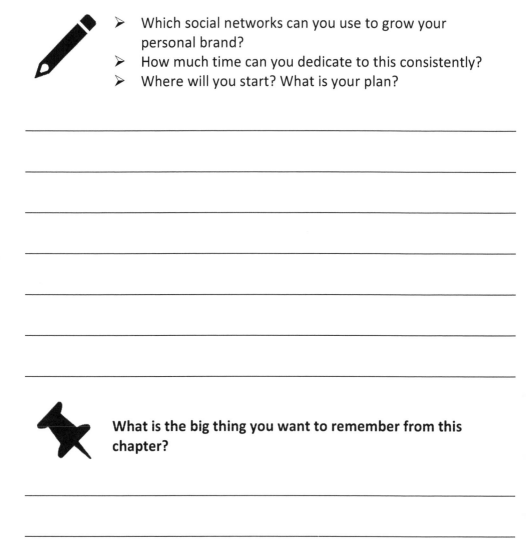

➢ Which social networks can you use to grow your personal brand?
➢ How much time can you dedicate to this consistently?
➢ Where will you start? What is your plan?

_____

_____

_____

_____

_____

_____

What is the big thing you want to remember from this chapter?

_____

_____

Go to www.LaunchYourself.com/book for your free action planner and bonus resources.

CHAPTER 16: BUILDING YOUR PERSONAL BRANDING PLAN

The ball is now in your court! It is time to take action and drive impact to grow your personal brand.

Complete and Review the Action Planner

Hopefully you've been completing the action planner throughout this book. This is your opportunity to step back and really think about what you want from your personal brand, how you want to position yourself, how you can build a strong brand, and deliberately plan out how you will bring your personal brand to life.

Remember that this isn't a one-and-done type of project. As you explore yourself and try different things with your brand you will start to change and refine it. Pay attention to the feedback that you get and be agile to adapt and incorporate what works (and what doesn't) into your strategy and execution.

It's perfectly okay if you don't have all of the answers right here and right now. I've struggled with completing some parts of my personal brand pyramid for YEARS (and I still don't love them). Get as close as you can and start executing. As you become more aware of your personal brand and look for feedback and signals you will refine and improve your brand over time.

Determine Your Resources

As you begin to move forward in your execution determine the resources that you have (both time and money) to execute. Many things take more time and effort than you realize. Once you execute something you still need to have capacity to analyze and optimize to grow your results.

Determine the resources that you have available as you decide how much to take on.

Build Your Personal Branding Plan

To initiate your personal brand, build a clear and time-oriented execution plan. Once you've decided which activities to take on, build out your action plan.

It is usually helpful to time your action plan into four buckets based on:

- Immediate
- 3 Months
- 6 – 9 Months
- Next year

Once an activity is on the horizon create more specific steps to execute so you are clear on what needs to happen when to get results. It is helpful to break down the steps so that you can be realistic about what is involved in the execution. Sometimes tasks that seem quick are actually more challenging, which can be uncovered by mapping out the steps.

Action:
If you've been completing the action planner through this book you should be ready to go and clear on your priorities.

Pro Tips to Get Started

Some of these have been mentioned in the book, but keep them in mind to maximize your results.

1) Don't get too caught up in perfection – get close enough and keep moving forward.
2) Just do it. Make the video. Write the article. Get over your inhibitions and fears. You've got this.
3) Do fewer things better. Master something before you move on to the next.
4) Be realistic about investments. Some things take more time and effort than expected, and you may hit technical issues.
5) The devil is in the details. Some details can make or break your success – make sure you nail the details that matter.
6) Great content is vital. Create excellent content that has value to your audience to break-through the clutter and get noticed in a more competitive landscape.
7) Test, test, test. If you aren't getting results or if the success of something really matters invest in testing to maximize your results.
8) Make time for analytics. Many people just execute, execute, execute. They don't step back to check that their efforts are working before they continue to invest.
9) Prioritize your efforts. We often focus on the wrong things and miss the things that matter most. *This is something I regularly kick myself for.*
10) #ThinkImpact in everything you do. Focus on what matters most.

BUILDING YOUR PERSONAL BRANDING PLAN

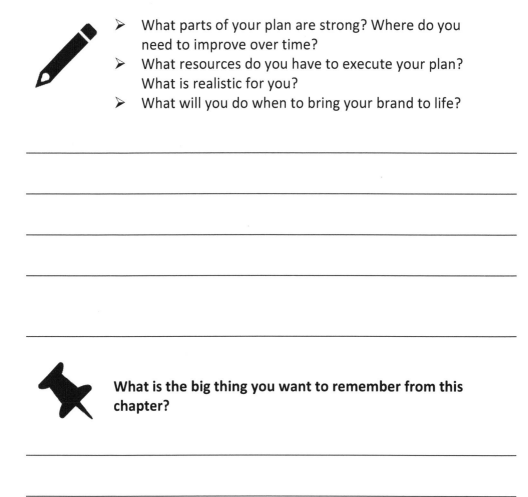

➤ What parts of your plan are strong? Where do you need to improve over time?
➤ What resources do you have to execute your plan? What is realistic for you?
➤ What will you do when to bring your brand to life?

_____

_____

_____

_____

_____

What is the big thing you want to remember from this chapter?

_____

_____

Go to www.LaunchYourself.com/book for your free action planner and bonus resources.

Want to take your social media and digital marketing skills to the next level? Go to **www.BootCampDigital.com** to see how we can help you succeed.

What We Offer at Boot Camp Digital:

- Online training courses from Beginner to Advanced
- Industry-recognized Certifications in Social Media, Digital Marketing, Content, SEO and more
- Live workshops across the U.S.
- Customized corporate team training globally
- Digital Marketing and Social Media consulting
- 1:1 Coaching and Strategic Planning

Connect with Us Online

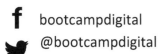 bootcampdigital
@bootcampdigital

 @bootcampdigital
Boot Camp Digital

Contact us for speaking, training, consulting, seminar or workshop opportunities at **info@bootcampdigital.com** or call us at **513-223-3878**.

About the Author

Krista Neher is the CEO of Boot Camp Digital, a bestselling author, an international speaker and a seasoned marketing executive. She has worked with leading companies like Google, P&G, General Mills, Nike, GE, The United States Senate, Prudential, Remax, and more. She has been a featured expert in the Wall Street Journal, New York Times, CNN, Associated Press, Wired Magazine, and more. Krista is passionate about social media and created one of the first accredited social media certification programs in the world.

Connect with Krista Online

f Krista.Neher.Pro

  @KristaNeher

🐦 @KristaNeher

in Krista Neher

Want to Work with Krista?

Krista works with a wide variety of businesses across industries and can work with you in a number of ways:

- Keynote presentations
- Workshops
- Breakout sessions
- Customized internal training programs
- 1:1 Coaching
- Executive training
- Corporate training
- Consulting
- Strategic planning

Contact Krista for speaking, training, consulting, seminar or workshop opportunities at **info@bootcampdigital.com** or call us at **513-223-3878.**

Made in the USA
San Bernardino,
CA

57702405R00120